Top 50 Social Studies Skills

for GED

SUCCESS

Reading Level:	**8+**
Category:	**GED Material**
Subcategory:	**GED–Social Studies**
Workbook Available:	
Teacher Guide Available:	
Part of a Series:	**Yes**
CD / CD ROM / DVD Available:	

KENNY TAMARKIN

Executive Editor: Linda Kwil
Cover Design: Tracey Harris-Sainz
Interior Design: Linda Chandler

Wright Group

ISBN: 0-07-704472-X
ISBN: 0-07-704473-8 (with CD-ROM)
ISBN-13

Send all inquiries to:
Wright Group/McGraw-Hill
130 E. Randolph Street, Suite 400
Chicago, IL 60601

2 3 4 5 6 7 8 9 POH 10 09 08 07

Table of Contents

Acknowledgments

The editor has made every effort to trace ownership of all copyrighted material and to secure the necessary permissions. Should there be a question regarding the use of any material, regret is hereby expressed for such error. Upon notification of any such oversight, proper acknowledgments will be made in future editions.

Map on page 7: Science Nobel Prize Winners © Matthew White. Reprinted by permission.

Map on page 8: Ski trails and lifts in Buck Hill. http://www.buckhill.com.

Maps on page 9: Prisoners of the Census. U.S. Prison Proliferation, 1900–2000. Reprinted by permission of Prison Policy Initiative, www.prisonpolicy.org.

Cartoon on page 10: "Progress Report." By permission of Steve Sack and Creators Syndicate, Inc.

Cartoon on page 11: "A caravan of California millionaires …" © The New Yorker Collection 1936 Carl Rose from cartoonbank.com. All rights reserved. Reprinted by permission.

Cartoon on page 11: "I like your looks, Ramsey." © The New Yorker Collection 1949 Alain from cartoonbank.com. All rights reserved. Reprinted by permission.

Cartoon on page 12: "Joe, these people say they want flesh-colored Band-Aids."© The New Yorker Collection 1963 William O'Brien from cartoonbank.com. All rights reserved. Reprinted by permission.

Cartoon on page 12: "Welcome aboard!" © The New Yorker Collection 1987 Gahan Wilson from cartoonbank.com. All rights reserved. Reprinted by permission.

Photograph on page 13: "Colored Admission 10¢." Courtesy of Library of Congress.

Graph on page 14: Drug use by U. S. High School Seniors. National Institute on Drug Abuse; other Federal Government Sources.

Graph on page 15 from the Chronology on the History of Slavery and Racism http://innercity.org/holt/slavechron. html, compiled from census data at the Geospatial and Statistical Data Center at the University of Virginia, http:// fisher.lib.virginia.edu/collections/stats/ histcensus. Reprinted by permission.

Graph on page 15: Change in Population in Indiana. Kelley School of Business. http://www.ibrc.indiana.edu.

Table on page 16: Patterns of World Urbanization. Reprinted by permission of the Population Reference Bureau.

Excerpt on page 43 from *The Fun of It, Random Records of My Own Flying and of Women in Aviation* by Amelia Earhart.

Excerpt on page 43 from "How Mark Felt Became 'Deep Throat'" by Bob Woodward, *The Washington Post*, June 2, 2005. © 2005, The Washington Post, reprinted with permission.

Excerpt on page 44 from *A People's History of the United States* by Howard Zinn.

Excerpt on page 45 from *Maude Adams: An Intimate Portrait* by Phyllis Robbins.

Excerpt on page 55 from the National Party submission to the South African Truth and Reconciliation Commission. http://www.doj.gov.za.

Excerpt on page 55 from the African National Congress to the South African Truth and Reconciliation Commission. http://www.doj.gov.za.

Excerpt on page 57 from "The Trail of Tears," *About North Georgia* by Golden Ink, http://ngeorgia.com. Reprinted by permission of Randy Golden.

Map on page 59 of the Silk Routes. http://www.globaled.org.

Map on page 60: Polar Ice Sheet. Courtesy of NASA.

Map on page 61: 1990 Life Expectancy © Matthew White. Reprinted by permission.

Map on page 62: Colorado Highway Map. World Sites Atlas (sitesatlas.com). Reprinted by permission.

Map on page 64: Map of Superfund sites in the United States. www.scorecard.org. Reprinted by permission.

Map on page 66: Urban Population Growth Map. World Resources Institute.

Map on page 67: Map of the last ancient forests of North America. Copyright 2002 Greenpeace/Global Forest Watch.

Map on page 68: World Ocean Floor Panorama by Bruce C. Heezen and Marie Tharp. © Copyright by Marie Tharp 1977/2003. Reproduced by permission of Marie Tharp Oceanographic Cartographer, One Washington Ave., South Nyack, New York, 10960.

Map on page 70: Persian Empire and Greece Map. http://www.livius.org. Reprinted by permission of Jona Lendering.

Map on page 70: Unpaid fines reach billions in some states. http://apnews.excite.com.

Map on page 72: Nepal Map. Courtesy of the University of Texas Libraries, The University of Texas at Austin.

Map on page 73: Casualties in WWII © Matthew White. Reprinted by permission.

Maps on page 73: Milwaukee Population and Milwaukee Light Maps. http://www. wisconline.com/greenmap/milwaukee

Map on page 74: Jerusalem crusader map. National Library of The Netherlands.

Map on page 75: Whale Map. Reprinted by permission of the Natural Resources Defense Council. www.savebiogems.org.

Table on page 111: 1998 United States Unintentional Injuries and Adverse Effects, ages 15–24, All Races, Both Sexes. Produced by: Office of Statistics and Programming, National Center for Injury Prevention and Control, CDC. Data Source: National Center for Health Statistics (NCHS) Vital Statistics Systems for numbers of deaths.

Graphs on page 112 of legal and illegal immigrants. Pew Hispanic Center. http://apnews.excite.com.

Graph on page 112: Teen sexual activity. 1995 National Survey of Family Growth and 1995 National Survey of Adolescent Males.

Graph on page 113: Sales of Illegal drugs in U.S. National Drug Intelligence Center. Office of National Drug Control Policy. *National Drug Threat Assessment 2005 Summary Report*, February 2005.

Graph on page 113: Extinction Threat. J. E. M. Baillie, C. Hilton-Taylor and S. N. Stuart (Editors) 2004. *2004 IUCN Red List of Threatened Species. A Global Species Assessment*. IUCN, Gland, Switzerland and Cambridge, UK. xxix. Reprinted by permission.

Graph on page 114: Smoking status by sex, persons aged 16 and over, NSW 1977 to 2002–03. http://www.health.nsw.gov.au.

Table on page 114: ABC News Invisible Primary March 23, 2006. http://abcnews.go.com.

Graph on page 115: Projections for Energy Consumption. Energy Information Administration.

Table on page 115: Personal computers per 1000 people. Reprinted with permission from *Encyclopædia Britannica*, © 2006 by Encyclopædia Britannica, Inc.

Graph on page 116: NAFTA Effect on Mexico. INEGI, Base de Información Ecomónica, February 2001. Ecomonic Policy Institute. http://www.epinet.org.

Table on page 116: Sub-Saharan Africa: HIV & AIDS statistics and features, in 2003 and 2005 from *AIDS epidemic update*, December 2005. 2003 and 2005 data reproduced by kind permission of UNAIDS (2005).

Graph on page 117: MLB salaries and income. EH.Net Encyclopedia. Reprinted by permission of EH.Net and Dr. Michael Haupert.

Table on page 118: Deaths from Drugs in U. S. National Institute on Drug Abuse and other Federal Government Sources.

Table on page 118: GNP per capita of China and the United States (normal U.S. $). Reprinted with permission from *Encyclopædia Britannica*, © 2006 by Encyclopædia Britannica, Inc.

Graph on page 119: Snapshots: Health Care Costs. This information was reprinted with permission from the Henry J. Kaiser Family Foundation. The Kaiser Family Foundation, based in Menlo Park, California, is a nonprofit, private operating foundation focusing on the major health care issues facing the nation and is not associated with Kaiser Permanente or Kaiser Industries.

Graph on page 120: U. S. Infant Mortality. Reprinted with permission from *Encyclopædia Britannica*, © 2006 by Encyclopædia Britannica, Inc.

Graph on page 120: Facts about Wealth that Every American Should Know. http://www.osjspm.org.

Graph on page 121: Foreign Aid. Global Issues - Sustainable Development. http://www.globalissues.org.

Table on page 121: Deforestation and Reforestation Rates. *National Forestry Action Programmes,* Update No. 32, July 1995. Reprinted by permission of Food and Agriculture Organization of the United Nations.

Cartoon on page 134: "Now, this complete, all-in-one model …" © The New Yorker Collection 1950 George Price from cartoonbank.com. All Rights Reserved. Reprinted by permission.

Cartoon on page 135: "Entering Hillsville." © The New Yorker Collection 1976 Dana Fradon from cartoonbank. com. All Rights Reserved. Reprinted by permission.

Cartoon on page 135: "It's an amazing coincidence …" © The New Yorker Collection 2000 James Stevenson from cartoonbank.com. All Rights Reserved. Reprinted by permission.

Cartoon on page 136: "Coastal Erosion." © Steve Kelley, *The New Orleans Time-Picayune.*

Cartoon on page 136: "Energy Independence." © 2006 Sandy Huffaker. All rights reserved.

Photograph on page 137: Pioneer family in Nebraska. Courtesy of U.S. National Archives & Records Administration.

Photograph on page 137: Children playing. The Granger Collection, New York.

Photograph on page 138: Flooded New Orleans. © AP/Wide World Photos.

Graph on page 139 from "Computing in Chile: The Jaguar of the Pacific Rim?", R. A. Baeza-Yates, D. A. Fuller, J. A. Pino, and S. E. Goodman. http://www.dcc.uchile.cl

Graph on page 139: Wheat exports 2003/2004. http://www.nationmaster.com.

Graph on page 140: Top Ten Cities of the year 1000. http://geography.about. com/library/weekly/aa011201c.htm

Graph on page 140: Murder by Firearms. http://www.nationmaster.com.

How to Use This Book

Test Overview

The GED Social Studies Test contains 50 multiple-choice questions, and you will be allowed 70 minutes to complete the test. You will need to be able to show that you can comprehend what you read, apply information to a new situation, analyze relationships among ideas or concepts, and make judgments about the material presented. The context of the test shows you as an acquirer, organizer, and user of information in your roles as an adult: citizen, family member, worker, and consumer.

Content areas covered on the test are the following:

- U.S. History 25%
- World History 15%
- Geography 15%
- Civics and Government 25%
- Economics 20%

About 40 percent of the questions will be based on visual text, such as graphs, tables, charts, maps, political cartoons, and photographs. Another 40 percent of the questions will be based on reading passages. The remaining 20 percent of the questions will refer to reading passages and visuals together.

About *Top 50 Social Studies Skills for GED Success*

Top 50 Social Studies Skills for GED Success is a short, test-directed course in GED social studies preparation. The 50 skills chosen are those most representative of the type and difficulty level of skills tested on the GED Social Studies Test. Each question in the Pretest addresses a particular skill. Guided instruction and follow-up questions for each skill are provided in the instruction section, pages 20–121.

Top 50 Social Studies Skills for GED Success is divided into four main sections:

- Pretest: 50 questions that check your understanding of core cognitive and contextual skills addressed on the GED Social Studies Test. These skills are chosen from subject areas identified by the GED Testing Service.
- Top 50 Skills Instruction: Instruction and follow-up practice on the 50 skills most likely to be addressed on the GED Social Studies Test. Additional practice questions increase your understanding and extend your knowledge.
- GED Posttest: A model GED test to check your readiness for the GED. Use the model to practice taking a GED test under test-like conditions.

Top 50 Social Studies Skills for GED Success is designed to be both student and instructor friendly, organizing for you in 50 lessons a core of social studies skills identified by the GED Testing Service. Each two-page skill lesson addresses a single skill and provides follow-up practice. One or more lessons can be completed in a single study period.

Top 50 Social Studies Skills for GED Success can be used in a variety of ways:

- student-directed self study
- one-on-one instruction
- group instruction

About the Pretest

This Pretest is an overview of 50 skills you are most likely to see addressed on the GED Social Studies Test. Questions come from the following National Council for Social Studies themes:

- Culture, people, and places (history, geography, and sociology)
- Time, continuity, and change (history)
- People, places, and environments (geography)
- Power, authority, and governance (civics and government)
- Production, distribution, and consumption (economics)
- Science, technology, and society (applications of social science)
- Global connections (history, geography, and economics)

Within these themes, the following traditional subject areas of social studies are covered:

- U.S. History
- World History
- Geography
- Civics and Government
- Economics

For the actual GED Social Studies Test, you will have 70 minutes to read the passages, graphs, maps, photos, cartoons, tables, and charts and answer 50 multiple-choice questions. However, this Pretest is not a timed test. In fact, you should take as much time as you need to answer each question. This Pretest is designed to help you identify specific skills and areas of understanding in which you need more practice.

Answer every question on this Pretest. If you are not sure of an answer, eliminate the obviously wrong answers and choose the most likely choice. Then put a question mark by the item number to note that you are guessing. You may return to this question later if you wish. On the actual GED Test, an unanswered question is counted as incorrect, so making a good guess is an important skill to develop.

When you are finished, turn to the Answer Key on page 144 to check your answers. Then use the Pretest Evaluation Chart on pages 18–19 to figure out which skills to focus on in the instruction section of the book (pages 20–121).

After working through the instruction section, take the Posttest on pages 124–141. Your success on the Posttest will indicate your readiness to take the actual GED Social Studies Test.

Pretest

Questions 1 and 2 refer to the following passage.

The 1960s were the great era of African independence. Cameroon, Togo, Mali, Senegal, Madagascar, Benin, Burkina Faso, Ivory Coast, Chad, Central African Republic, Republic of the Congo, Gabon, Mauritania, and Algeria all won their independence from France. The Democratic Republic of the Congo, Burundi, and Rwanda became independent of Belgium. Somalia, Nigeria, Sierra Leone, Tanzania, Uganda, Kenya, Malawi, Zambia, Gambia, Botswana, Lesotho, Mauritius, and Swaziland gained independence from the United Kingdom. Equatorial Guinea became independent of Spain. While most of these transitions of power were peaceful, some were a result of protracted struggles.

1 Which of the following is the main idea of this passage?

  ① The 1960s were the great era of African independence.
  ② France and the United Kingdom were colonial powers.
  ③ Rwanda became independent of Belgium.
  ④ Most African countries became independent peacefully.
  ⑤ Some African countries fought for independence.

2 What is the writer's point of view about African nations becoming independent?

  ① The African nations were not ready for independence from the colonial powers.
  ② The colonial powers ran away from their responsibilities toward Africa.
  ③ The independence of so many African nations was an important event.
  ④ Africa was fragmented into too many small and weak independent nations.
  ⑤ Independence was a crucial step in the economic development of Africa.

Questions 3 and 4 refer to the following passage.

A little over a century ago, horses were still an important mode of local transportation. While trains and trolleys were becoming more common, many people still rode on horseback to travel from place to place. They also used horse-drawn carriages. Horse-drawn wagons were used to deliver many products to individual businesses and homes. Horses were used to pull many types of machinery and equipment on farms.

The invention of the automobile in the late nineteenth century changed local transportation. By the early twentieth century, more and more people started to travel in automobiles and buses. Trucks began to deliver most products, and tractors started to be used on many farms.

3 What conclusion about the early twentieth century can you draw from this passage?

  ① People came up with new uses for horses.
  ② People regretted the replacement of the horse by machines.
  ③ The need for blacksmiths, who made horseshoes, declined.
  ④ Barns were converted to condominiums and apartments.
  ⑤ Horses were banned from many urban areas.

4 What value is being highlighted in this passage?

  ① humane treatment of animals
  ② productivity and efficiency
  ③ love of novelty and change
  ④ preservation of traditions
  ⑤ better sanitary conditions

Questions 5 and 6 refer to the following passage.

The euro is the currency of twelve European Union countries: Belgium, Germany, Greece, Spain, France, Ireland, Italy, Luxembourg, the Netherlands, Austria, Portugal, and Finland. Euro banknotes and coins have been in circulation since January 1, 2002. They are now a part of daily life for more than 300 million Europeans living in the euro area. International acceptance of the euro continues to grow. In 2003, more than 50 percent of countries throughout the world had another currency in circulation in addition to their own. In 87 percent of those countries, the dollar is that currency. In 27 percent of the countries, the euro is in circulation. As the value of the euro relative to the dollar continues to improve, its international acceptance is likely to improve as well.

5 Which is an implication of the passage?

  ① The dollar is threatened by the growing acceptance of the euro.
  ② The European economy depends on acceptance of the euro.
  ③ In some nations, the dollar and the euro are both in circulation.
  ④ In a few years, the euro will be the world's dominant currency.
  ⑤ The euro and the dollar are the only two currencies used in other countries.

6 What is currency?

  ① credit
  ② something new
  ③ trade
  ④ value
  ⑤ money

Questions 7 and 8 refer to the following passage, which was written before the Revolutionary War.

The colonies are now in a state of revolt and rebellion against their rightful ruler. The British legislation is determined to bring them back to their rightful government. The most generous offers have been made to them—a redress of grievances, an exemption from taxes, and a free trade. These liberal terms would make America the happiest, freest, and most flourishing country in the world. But the American Congress has rejected these terms. The Congress, therefore, is responsible for all the calamities which America now suffers, and for all those greater calamities which it will probably suffer in the course of this unnatural contest.

7 What is the writer trying to convince the reader to believe?

  ① The independent United States should be an ally of the British.
  ② The Americans were justified in rebelling against the British.
  ③ The American Congress should have the authority to govern.
  ④ America is the world's happiest, freest, and most flourishing nation.
  ⑤ The Americans should end their rebellion against their king.

8 The writer is most likely

  ① a modern historian evaluating British offers to the colonies
  ② a descendant of someone who fought against the Revolution
  ③ a conservative member of the Continental Congress
  ④ a British sympathizer at the time of the American Revolution
  ⑤ an American colonist after the settling of Jamestown

Questions 9 and 10 refer to the following passage.

The experiences and motivations of common soldiers on both sides during the Civil War were surprisingly similar. Northern and Southern soldiers were influenced by patriotism and nationalism. However, Northern soldiers felt they were fighting to preserve the Union, while Southern soldiers felt they were fighting for the South's right to self-government. Both claimed that they were fighting for liberty, though they had a different understanding of what that meant.

In the early years of the Civil War, slavery was not an issue on either side, at least for white soldiers. Most common Confederate soldiers owned no slaves, so they did not care whether slavery survived. Northern soldiers were more interested in preserving the Union.

Both sides used more accurate and powerful weapons than had ever been used in war before. As a result, hundreds of thousands on both sides were wounded or killed. But disease was the greatest enemy to both sides. Two men died from disease for every one that died as a result of battle. Hygiene and diet both were usually awful.

However, as the war went on, conditions for the Confederate soldiers got far worse. The South was not able to provide its troops with sufficient food, clothing, and other supplies, as the North continued to do.

9 What was one important difference between Union and Confederate soldiers?

  ① Union soldiers owned more slaves than Confederate soldiers.
  ② Confederate soldiers fought for the right to secede from the U.S.
  ③ Union soldiers believed in liberty while Confederates did not.
  ④ Many more Confederate soldiers died from disease and wounds.
  ⑤ Confederate soldiers had better hygiene than Union soldiers.

10 Which of the following is most similar to the description of Union and Confederate soldiers?

  ① the two top baseball teams meeting in the World Series
  ② Hutus killing over 500,000 Tutsis during the Rwandan genocide
  ③ European villagers being plundered by raiding Vikings in the Middle Ages
  ④ British and French soldiers fighting during the Napoleonic Wars
  ⑤ American cavalry and Indian warriors during the Indian Wars

Questions 11 and 12 refer to the following passage.

The United States changed warfare forever when it dropped the first atomic bomb on Hiroshima on August 6, 1945. The bomb destroyed 68 percent of the city and another 24 percent was damaged. Over 60,000 people were killed and thousands of others were poisoned by the radiation. A second bomb was dropped on Nagasaki just three days later.

There continues to be a debate about whether dropping the bombs was necessary. The Japanese surrendered on August 14, just five days after the second bomb was dropped. Records show that since May, Japan had been considering surrender, though the leaders of the army resisted making that decision. The atomic bombs made it clear that no matter how brave Japanese soldiers were, they could not prevail. Since the Japanese army could now save face, they were able to accept the surrender. If the bomb had not been used, the Allies would have had to invade Japan, possibly resulting in an even greater loss of life and property.

11 Which of the statements in the passage is not adequately supported by facts?

① The United States changed warfare forever by using the atomic bomb.
② The first atomic bomb used in warfare was dropped on Hiroshima.
③ Over 60,000 people were killed in Hiroshima by the atomic bomb.
④ The Japanese army had delayed the surrender of Japan before the bombing.
⑤ The Japanese surrendered eight days after the bombing of Hiroshima.

12 According to the passage, all of the following were causes of Japanese surrender except

① the atomic bomb allowing them to save face when they surrendered
② the huge loss of life as a result of the two atomic bombs
③ the Japanese realizing for months that they could not win the war
④ the Japanese inability to fight as bravely and well as the Americans
⑤ the Allies moving closer to an inevitable invasion of Japan

Questions 13 and 14 refer to the following quotes from the Russian Revolution.

"I am an opponent of the Bolsheviks. I consider them enemies of my country. I know that they will bring the greatest suffering upon the people. . . . But if I were asked whether I regretted the revolution, I would say no. And whatever my personal fate—if I were asked whether I'd live through the revolution again, I would say yes."
—Andrei Shingarev, former minister of the Russian Constitutional Democratic party, from his prison diary

"We need the real, nationwide terror which reinvigorates the country and through which the Great French Revolution achieved glory."
—Vladimir Lenin, Russian Bolshevik leader

13 Which of the following character traits does Shingarev display in his statement that Lenin does not?

① ruthlessness
② weakness
③ selfishness
④ regretfulness
⑤ concern for others

14 Which of the following is an unstated assumption of Lenin?

① Democracy will lead to a better, more just society.
② Total destruction is the best path to greatness.
③ The Russian Revolution should copy the French Revolution.
④ His nation needs to give power to the people.
⑤ The nation needs to follow the orders of a great leader.

Questions 15 and 16 refer to the following passage.

On June 28, 1989, Slobodan Milosevic made a speech in Kosovo to mark the six hundredth anniversary of the Battle of Kosovo. In that battle, the Turks defeated the Serbs, but the Serbs still consider that battle to be the beginning of the nation of Serbia.

Even though 90 percent of the people who live in Kosovo are ethnic Albanians, Milosevic was only speaking to ethnic Serbs. The Republic of Serbia was the dominant republic of Yugoslavia, and ethnic Serbs made up more than 40 percent of the nation's population. Despite that, many Serbians felt that they were treated unfairly in Yugoslavia. Milosevic fanned that discontent in his speech. He said, "We are being again engaged in battles and are facing battles. They are not armed battles, although such things cannot be excluded yet. Let the memory of Kosovo heroism live forever! Long live Serbia! Long live Yugoslavia! Long live peace and brotherhood among peoples!"

His listeners understood that the memory of Kosovo heroism was the memory of Serbian nationalism. They understood that Milosevic meant to return Kosovo to the Serbs and to build a greater Serbia on the ruins of a collapsing Yugoslavia.

15 Some supporters of Milosevic claim that his Kosovo speech was misunderstood. They claimed that he was supporting the unity of all the people of Serbia. What evidence is there in the passage to support this claim?

(1) He wanted to remember the heroism of the Serbs six hundred years ago.
(2) He made the speech in Kosovo, where 90 percent of the people were Albanians.
(3) He said that we are being again engaged in battles and are facing battles.
(4) When he made his speech, almost his entire audience was ethnic Serbs.
(5) In his speech he said, "Long live Yugoslavia! Long live peace and brotherhood."

16 Milosevic argued that Serbia had a right to Kosovo. What was the most important logical problem with that argument?

(1) The Battle of Kosovo occurred six hundred years ago.
(2) Kosovo was the historic homeland for the Serbs.
(3) Serbs made up only 10 percent of the population of Kosovo.
(4) Serbia was still a part of the nation of Yugoslavia.
(5) The Turks had defeated the Serbs at the Battle of Kosovo.

Questions 17 and 18 refer to the following passage.

Nationalism is devotion to the interests or culture of one's nation. A nationalist believes that the goals and interests of his nation are more important than the goals and interests of humanity as a whole. He thinks that the nation is the fundamental social unit. Membership in a nation can be determined by shared language, culture, heritage, or values. An extreme nationalist believes that any action is permissible if it is in the interest of the nation.

17 All of the following are examples of nationalism except

  ① Poland's successful effort to join the European Union

  ② Gandhi leading India to independence through non-violent action

  ③ the Nazis rearming Germany and invading their neighbors

  ④ Basque separatists fighting Spain for years to gain independence for their homeland

  ⑤ the United States taking territory from Mexico in order to fulfill its Manifest Destiny

18 Which of the following is an opinion?

  ① Uncontrolled nationalism led to great death and suffering in the twentieth century.

  ② Nationalism can often lead to war and should be opposed by reasonable people.

  ③ In the nineteenth century, nationalism was a factor in the unification of Italy.

  ④ A nationalist would likely be suspicious of the International Court of Justice.

  ⑤ American nationalists in the U.S. insist that English be our shared language.

Questions 19 and 20 refer to the following map.

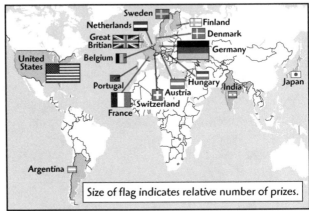

SCIENCE NOBEL PRIZE WINNERS, 2ND QUARTER OF THE 20TH CENTURY

Size of flag indicates relative number of prizes.

19 Which of the following information about the second quarter of the twentieth century cannot be obtained from this map?

  ① The United States had the world's best science education system.

  ② Most of the world's important scientific research was in the U.S. and Europe.

  ③ Important scientific advances happened in many European countries.

  ④ The United States had more Nobel Prize winners than any other nation.

  ⑤ Great Britain had the third largest number of Nobel Prize winners.

20 Which of the following is an implication that can be drawn from this map?

  ① The U.S. and Europe were centers for innovation in the world during the second quarter of the twentieth century.

  ② The scientific advances of the second quarter of the twentieth century helped make modern war more deadly.

  ③ Africa was seen as a promising new location for scientific research at the end of the second quarter of the twentieth century.

  ④ The United States and Germany fought for world supremacy in the second quarter of the twentieth century.

  ⑤ Scientists moved freely between labs in the U.S. and Europe during the second quarter of the twentieth century.

Questions 21 and 22 refer to the following map of the Buck Hill ski area in Minnesota.

BUCK HILL TRAIL MAP

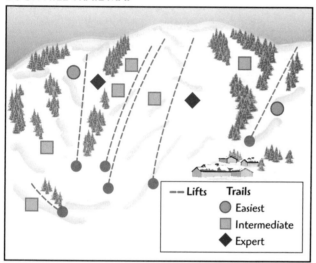

21 What is the purpose of this map?

① to help skiers find the Buck Hill ski area
② to compare Buck Hill to other ski mountains in the area
③ to provide a useful trail guide for hikers in the summer
④ to help skiers select lifts and trails right for their ability
⑤ to help skiers locate their lodging relative to the mountain

22 If you were an expert skier, which lifts would you want to use for most of the day?

① lifts 1 and 2
② lifts 2 and 3
③ lifts 3 and 4
④ lifts 4 and 5
⑤ lifts 2 and 5

Questions 23 and 24 refer to the following map of the Age of Discovery.

SPAIN'S AND PORTUGAL'S EXPLORATIONS DURING THE AGE OF DISCOVERY

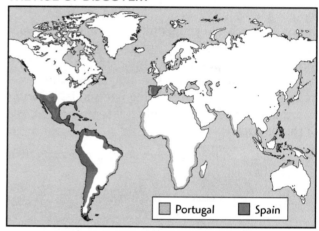

23 The greatest contrast between Portugal's and Spain's explorations during the Age of Discovery is

① the distance of their travels
② the amount of area explored
③ their explorations in the East Indies
④ their explorations in South America
⑤ their explorations in Africa

24 There is enough information in this map to determine all of the following except

① Spain explored the most territory in the Americas
② Portugal explored the most territory in Africa
③ the British replaced Spain and Portugal as the leading colonizer
④ most early explorations were along the coasts of the world
⑤ the European explorers had access to the Atlantic Ocean

Questions 25, 26, and 27 refer to the following maps.

U.S. PRISONS 1940–2000

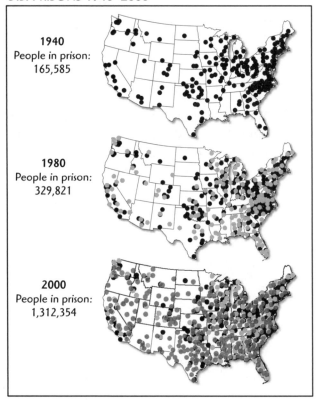

1940
People in prison:
165,585

1980
People in prison:
329,821

2000
People in prison:
1,312,354

25 How would a planner in the rapidly growing western state of Nevada apply the information in this series of maps?

1. He or she would see an increased need and start the process to build more prisons.
2. He or she would support laws to slow migration from crime-ridden eastern states.
3. He or she would ask for stricter sentencing guidelines so more people were in prison.
4. He or she would try to set up agreements to send Nevada prisoners to out-of-state prisons.
5. He or she would try to convince local communities that they should welcome a new prison.

26 Which of the following is an opinion about this series of maps?

1. The number of prisons in the U.S. increased throughout the twentieth century.
2. The incarceration rate in the U.S. increased throughout the twentieth century.
3. The number of Americans being held in U.S. prisons is a national disgrace.
4. The eastern half of the U.S. has most of the prisons in the country.
5. The northern Great Plains have fewer prisons than any other region in the U.S.

27 Which of the following is a conclusion you can draw from this series of maps?

1. Throughout the twentieth century, the number of lawbreakers increased.
2. Many criminals in the U.S. have been able to avoid punishment.
3. The number of prisons in the U.S. peaked in 2000 and is now in decline.
4. It is likely that the number of prisons in the U.S. is still growing.
5. Building more prisons has made the United States a safer place.

Questions 28 and 29 refer to the following political cartoon.

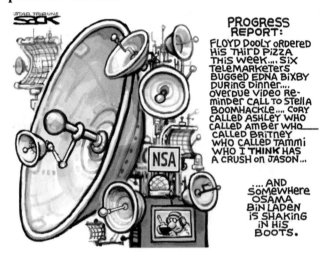

PROGRESS REPORT:
FLOYD DOOLY ORDERED HIS THIRD PIZZA THIS WEEK.... SIX TELEMARKETERS BUGGED EDNA BIXBY DURING DINNER.... OVERDUE VIDEO REMINDER CALL TO STELLA BOOMHACKLE.... CORY CALLED ASHLEY WHO CALLED AMBER WHO CALLED BRITNEY WHO CALLED TAMMI WHO I THINK HAS A CRUSH ON JASON...

....AND SOMEWHERE OSAMA BIN LADEN IS SHAKING IN HIS BOOTS.

In May 2006, it was revealed that the National Security Agency (NSA) had been secretly collecting the phone records of ordinary Americans. They claimed that this was supposed to help in the war on terror.

28 What is the main idea of this political cartoon?

① Terrorists are being successfully tracked down because of the NSA spying program.
② The phone records of Americans contain a lot of interesting personal information.
③ In order to catch Osama bin Laden, we need to increase support for the NSA.
④ The NSA practice of collecting phone records is totally misguided and ineffective.
⑤ Americans need to be careful whom they call because the NSA collects their phone records.

29 Which of the following is a fact that this cartoon is commenting on?

① The NSA is closing in on terrorists by using effective information gathering.
② The NSA is gathering enormous amounts of data on the phone calls of Americans.
③ The people who object to the NSA collecting phone records have something to hide.
④ The United States is not doing all it can to track down and capture Osama bin Laden.
⑤ Our right to privacy has been violated in an attempt to assure a false sense of security.

Questions 30 and 31 refer to the following political cartoon.

A CARAVAN OF CALIFORNIA MILLIONAIRES, FLEEING EASTWARD FROM THE STATE INCOME TAX, ENCAMPS FOR THE NIGHT IN HOSTILE WISCONSIN TERRITORY

30 Which of the following is most likely the historical period of this cartoon?

  ① during colonial times before the American Revolution

  ② during the westward expansion of the United States

  ③ during the early years of the automobile around 1900

  ④ during the Great Depression in the 1930s

  ⑤ during the economic boom of the 1990s

31 Where does the humor in this cartoon come from?

  ① the image of millionaires circling their limousines like pioneers circling their wagons

  ② the exaggeration of the length of the limousines to make them look more expensive

  ③ the idea that millionaires would actually move to avoid paying their share of taxes

  ④ the assertion that millionaires need protection from the anger of ordinary people

  ⑤ the millionaires having a fancy catered dinner out in the middle of the prairie

Questions 32 and 33 refer to the following political cartoon.

"I like your looks, Ramsey. You're hired."

32 What is an implication of this cartoon?

  ① It's very important to dress well for an interview.

  ② Employers tend to hire people who are like themselves.

  ③ There is no reason to have affirmative action in hiring.

  ④ A firm handshake can make you appear confident.

  ⑤ Always research a company before you apply for a job there.

33 What is the cartoonist's point of view of the hiring situation?

  ① He is sympathetic of people who are job hunting.

  ② He appreciates successful and friendly businessmen.

  ③ He wants to show unintentional discrimination at work.

  ④ He wants to give the reader an inside look at how corporations work.

  ⑤ He appreciates the hiring system that helps companies be effective.

Questions 34 and 35 refer to the following political cartoon.

"Joe, these people say they want flesh-colored Band-Aids."

34 What is the unstated assumption that this cartoon is addressing?

(1) The customer is always right.
(2) A customer should be served right away.
(3) Workers need to be able to work with different people.
(4) Stores do not always stock enough variety of products.
(5) The color of flesh is the color of a Caucasian.

35 What does the cartoonist do to persuade you?

(1) He shows the salesperson as overwhelmed.
(2) He has the customers wearing traditional dress.
(3) All the customers are innocently expecting to be served.
(4) The customers are crowding around the salesman.
(5) The customers appear to be despairing of ever getting served.

Questions 36 and 37 refer to the following political cartoon.

"Welcome aboard!"

36 What does the cartoonist expect you to know in order to understand the cartoon?

(1) Business owners can often dress and behave strangely.
(2) A new worker expects to be greeted by his supervisor.
(3) A good worker needs to be able to adjust to surprises.
(4) A pirate is a ruthless plunderer who takes what he can.
(5) Every company develops its own corporate culture.

37 What will the new employee most likely have to do on the job?

(1) steal and take advantage of others for the company
(2) give the company a more respectable face for the public
(3) work hard, honestly, and responsibly for the good of his customers
(4) help his supervisor look and behave more up-to-date
(5) take care of those details that his boss might have overlooked

Questions 38 and 39 refer to the following advertisement from the early twentieth century.

ADVERTISEMENT

An Ideal Vacation
. . . *without leaving the city*

Soon the trains and boats will be filled with thousands seeking fresh air and outdoor life, only to return to their flats or apartments after a few short days of the week.

Shorewood Park right in San Francisco, offers you an "All-year-round Vacation." Large lots, nearby and close are the Golf Links and Ocean Beach. Shorewood PRICES are about the same as you would pay in the suburbs. Large lots $35 to $40 per front foot. Bungalows are $40 to $45 per month.

JONES & NASK
468 PINE AVENUE
PHONE LARAMIE 4621

38 How did the advertiser want the reader to apply the information given in the above advertisement?

(1) call to plan their next vacation
(2) stay in the city instead of moving away
(3) buy land or a home in Shorewood Park
(4) go to the beach on their next vacation
(5) spend more money than they can afford

39 Which of the following was not a likely effect of this advertisement?

(1) Some readers called the office for more information.
(2) Other neighborhoods suffered as people moved to Shorewood Park.
(3) Some readers decided to buy land or homes in Shorewood Park.
(4) Jones and Nask probably placed more advertisements.
(5) Happy new residents ended up spending years in the community.

Questions 40 and 41 are based on the following photograph.

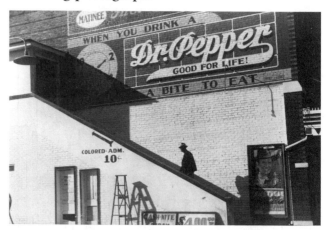

40 All of the following could be reasons the photographer took this photograph except

(1) to show the injustice and indignity of segregation
(2) to show the second class treatment of African Americans
(3) to preserve a record of the place and time in the South
(4) to create a powerful image of discrimination
(5) to show that separate but equal could be a reality

41 Which of the following values is illustrated by this photograph?

(1) Southern hospitality
(2) American capitalism
(3) democracy in action
(4) entertainment
(5) separation of the races

Questions 42 and 43 are based on the following line graph.

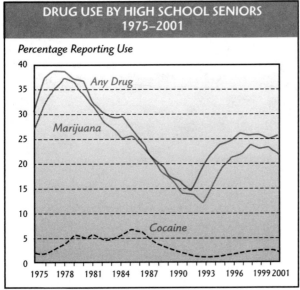

DRUG USE BY HIGH SCHOOL SENIORS
1975–2001

Percentage Reporting Use

Any Drug

Marijuana

Cocaine

1975 1978 1981 1984 1987 1990 1993 1996 1999 2001

Source: Monitoring the Future Study.

42 Which of the following is a trend in drug use by high school seniors during the period from 1975 to 2001 that is supported by the graph?

① There was a decrease in the use of most drugs throughout the 1980s.
② Cocaine use decreased throughout the 1980s before being level in the 1990s.
③ Marijuana use decreased throughout the 1980s and 1990s.
④ There was a surge in overall drug use from 1987 to 2001.
⑤ Throughout the 1980s cocaine was replacing marijuana as the most used drug.

43 Some people believe that marijuana use should be legalized. If that happened, what would be the most likely effect?

① The percentage of high school seniors reporting illegal drug use would dramatically drop.
② The percentage of high school seniors reporting the use of cocaine would dramatically rise.
③ The percentage of high school seniors reporting any illegal drug use would stay about the same.
④ The percentage of high school seniors using marijuana would dramatically drop.
⑤ The percentage of high school seniors using marijuana would approach 100 percent.

Questions 44 and 45 are based on the following bar graph.

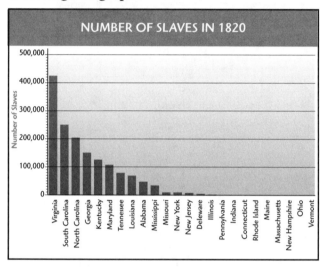

NUMBER OF SLAVES IN 1820

44. Which of the following best states the main idea of the above graph?

① Virginia had more slaves than any other state in 1820.
② In 1820, the northern states of New York and New Jersey still had slaves.
③ By 1820, there were no slaves in any of the New England states.
④ The number of slaves was rapidly increasing in the South in the 1820s.
⑤ In 1820, almost all slaves in the U.S. lived in the South.

45. Suppose that you were a slave in North Carolina in 1820, and you were planning to flee slavery by using the Underground Railroad. If you had seen this graph, where would you most want to reach?

① Mexican-controlled Texas
② the Spanish colony of Florida
③ the Middle Atlantic state of New Jersey
④ the border state of Kentucky
⑤ the New England state of Connecticut

Questions 46 and 47 are based on the following bar graph.

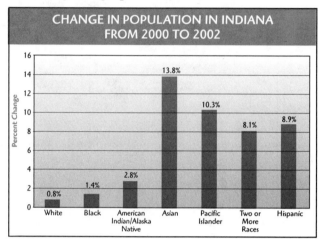

CHANGE IN POPULATION IN INDIANA FROM 2000 TO 2002

46. Which of the following is an implication of the above graph?

① Indiana will have fewer white residents in the future.
② African Americans will remain the second largest racial group.
③ Indiana will have a more diverse population in the future.
④ Asians are going to become the largest racial group in Indiana.
⑤ The percentage of whites in the state will grow slowly.

47. In order to determine whether Hispanics will ever be likely to outnumber African Americans in Indiana, all the additional information is needed except

① the average per capita income for each group
② the projected changes in migration to and from the state
③ the current total number of each group
④ the projected death rate for each group
⑤ the projected birth rate for each group

Questions 48, 49, and 50 are based on the following table.

TOP 10 LARGEST URBAN AREAS (IN MILLIONS) 1950, 2000, 2015								
1950			**2000**			**2015**		
Rank	Urban Area	Population	Rank	Urban Area	Population	Rank	Urban Area	Population
1.	New York, USA	12.3	1.	Tokyo, Japan	26.4	1.	Tokyo, Japan	26.4
2.	London, England	8.7	2.	Mexico City, Mexico	18.4	2.	Bombay, India	26.1
3.	Tokyo, Japan	6.9	3.	Bombay, India	18.0	3.	Lagos, Nigeria	23.2
4.	Paris, France	5.4	4.	São Paulo, Brazil	17.8	4.	Dhaka, Bangladesh	21.1
5.	Moscow, Russia	5.4	5.	New York, USA	16.6	5.	São Paulo, Brazil	20.4
6.	Shanghai, China	5.3	6.	Lagos, Nigeria	13.4	6.	Karachi, Pakistan	19.2
7.	Essen, Germany	5.3	7.	Los Angeles, USA	13.1	7.	Mexico City, Mexico	19.2
8.	Buenos Aires, Argentina	5.0	8.	Calcutta, India	12.9	8.	New York, USA	17.4
9.	Chicago, USA	4.9	9.	Shanghai, China	12.9	9.	Jakarta, Indonesia	17.3
10.	Calcutta, India	4.4	10.	Buenos Aires, Argentina	12.6	10.	Calcutta, India	4.4

Source: United Nations, *World Urbanization Prospects, The 1999 Revision.*

48 Which of the following is not an unstated assumption for the above table?

① It is a sign of prosperity for an urban area to gain population.
② Large urban areas will stabilize in developed countries.
③ The United Nations is a reliable source for population data.
④ It is possible to accurately predict population growth.
⑤ It was possible to get an accurate count in these urban areas.

49 The table gives evidence for all of the following contrasts except

① Over time the largest urban areas are getting larger.
② The developing world will have most of the largest urban areas.
③ Tokyo will remain among the world's largest areas until 2015.
④ London is now a less important urban area compared to Mexico City.
⑤ Dhaka is projected to be one of the world's fastest growing urban areas.

50 What is a value that might be tracked by the information in this table?

   ① commitment to find a better life for oneself and one's family

   ② pride in living in one of the world's largest urban centers

   ③ reverence for traditional customs and relationships

   ④ devotion to one's religious and spiritual beliefs

   ⑤ courage to move from a rural to an urban lifestyle

Pretest Evaluation Chart

After you complete the Pretest, check your answers with the Answer Key on page 144. Then use this chart to figure out which skills you need to focus on in the instruction section of the book. In column 1, circle the number of each question you missed. The second, third, and fourth columns tell you the name and number of the skill and its page numbers in the instruction section of this book. Focus your preparation on these skills. After you complete your study of each skill, put a check in the final column.

Question Number	Skill Name	Skill	Pages	Completed ✔
6	Restating Information	1	20–21	
1	Summarizing the Main Idea	2	22–23	
5	Identifying Implications	3	24–25	
17	Applying Given Ideas	4	26–29	
10	Applying Remembered Ideas	5	30–31	
18	Distinguishing Facts from Opinions and Hypotheses	6	32–33	
3	Drawing Conclusions	7	34–35	
7	Recognizing Persuasive Language	8	36–37	
14	Recognizing Unstated Assumptions	9	38–39	
12	Identifying Cause and Effect Relationships	10	40–41	
2	Recognizing the Writer's Point of View	11	42–43	
8	Recognizing the Historical Context of a Text	12	44–45	
9	Identifying Comparisons and Contrasts	13	46–47	
15	Judging Information	14	48–49	
4	Recognizing Values	15	50–51	
11	Judging the Adequacy of Facts	16	52–53	
13	Comparing and Contrasting Different Viewpoints	17	54–55	
16	Identifying Faulty Reasoning	18	56–57	
19	Restating Map Information	19	58–59	
20	Identifying Implications	20	60–61	
22	Applying Map Information	21	62–63	
21	Identifying the Purpose and Use of a Map	22	64–65	
23	Identifying Comparisons and Contrasts	23	66–67	
25	Applying Given Ideas	24	68–69	
24	Judging the Adequacy of Facts	25	70–71	
27	Drawing Conclusions	26	72–73	
26	Distinguishing Fact from Opinion	27	74–75	
28	Summarizing the Main Idea	28	76–77	

Question Number	Skill Name	Skill	Pages	Completed ✔
32	Identifying Implications	29	78–79	
36	Applying Remembered Ideas	30	80–81	
38	Applying Given Ideas	31	82–83	
29	Distinguishing Fact from Opinion	32	84–85	
35	Recognizing Persuasive Information	33	86–87	
40	Understanding the Photographer's or Cartoonist's Purpose	34	88–89	
34	Recognizing Unstated Assumptions	35	90–91	
39	Identifying Cause and Effect Relationships	36	92–93	
33	Recognizing the Cartoonist's or Photographer's Point of View	37	94–95	
30	Recognizing Historical Context	38	96–97	
31	Identifying Comparisons and Contrasts	39	98–99	
41	Recognizing Values	40	100–101	
37	Determining the Implications and Effects of Values	41	102–103	
42	Recognizing a Trend in Data	42	104–105	
44	Summarizing the Main Idea	43	106–107	
46	Identifying Implications	44	108–109	
45	Applying Information Given	45	110–111	
48	Recognizing Unstated Assumptions	46	112–113	
47	Judging the Adequacy of Facts	47	114–115	
43	Identifying Cause and Effect Relationships	48	116–117	
49	Identifying Comparisons and Contrasts	49	118–119	
50	Recognizing Values	50	120–121	

Restating Information

Restating information means using different words than you read in a passage to express an idea or describe something from that passage. For example, Juan read in the sports section of the newspaper that the manager of the local baseball team was relieved of his duties. He told his friend Joshua, "Did you hear that the manager was fired?" Juan has used his own words, but he has clearly and accurately restated what he read.

Read the following paragraph. In your own words, how would you describe how the Revolutions of 1848 ended?

> The Revolutions of 1848 created political upheaval across Europe. The revolutions began in France with the overthrow of King Louis Philippe. They then spread to Italy, the Austrian Empire, and Germany. None of the revolutions led to any permanent changes, and most were violently suppressed within a few months.

The passage says that the Revolutions of 1848 "began in France with the overthrow of King Louis Philippe." In other words, the government of France was changed by force.

The last sentence states that "most were violently suppressed." In other words, the Revolutions of 1848 were ended by force. They did not end as a result of a democratic process.

Reading Selection

After some 70 years of rule by the Institutional Revolutionary Party (PRI), a new party and government have come to power in Mexico. The PRI had based its long-term standing on an adversarial relationship with the United States. It has now been replaced. Elected in 2000, Vicente Fox represents the conservative National Action Party (PAN). The PAN had long been the organized political enemy of the controlling PRI. As president, Fox has vowed not only to change his country's domestic policies (for example, by reducing rampant corruption), but also to strengthen U.S.-Mexico relations.

❶ Given the information in the reading selection, what kind of a relationship did the PRI maintain with the United States?

_____

❷ What do a country's domestic policies deal with?

_____

GED Practice

Questions 1 and 2 refer to the following passage.

Led by Chairman Alan Greenspan, the Federal Reserve's Open Market Committee decided today to keep its target for the federal funds rate at 1 percent. This action keeps this key interest rate at a historic low.

The Committee continues to believe that by keeping interest rates low, it is providing important ongoing support to economic activity. The economic evidence accumulated over the past month confirms that spending is steady, and the labor market appears to be stabilizing. Business pricing power and increases in core consumer prices remain muted.

1 What is meant by "the labor market appears to be stabilizing"?

  ① The number of jobs is growing rapidly.
  ② Unemployed people cannot find new jobs.
  ③ Workers are changing jobs more frequently.
  ④ The balance between job seekers and available jobs is steady.
  ⑤ Workers are finding a greater choice for new jobs.

2 What is another way of saying that "business pricing power and increases in core consumer prices remain muted"?

  ① Companies are trying to be quiet about their price increases.
  ② Sellers have increased power to set prices to new levels.
  ③ There has been very little change in the prices of items.
  ④ Businesses and consumers are struggling to control prices.
  ⑤ There has been consistent strong inflation in the economy.

Questions 3 and 4 refer to the following passage.

In the early twentieth century, a group of journalists emerged who were committed to exposing the social, economic, and political problems of industrial life. In 1906, they were nicknamed "muckrakers" by President Theodore Roosevelt. He borrowed the word from John Bunyan's story *Pilgrim's Progress*. The story spoke of a man with a "muck-rake in his hand" who raked filth rather than look up to nobler things. Roosevelt recognized the muckrakers' key role in showing the need for progressive reform, as long as they knew when to "stop raking the muck" and avoid stirring up radical unrest.

Muckraking grew out of two related developments of the era—the changing of journalism and the reform impulse. The muckrakers represented a new group of educated reporters. They saw themselves as scientists objectively reporting the conditions and problems of modern industrial society. Most of their articles focused on business and political corruption.

The muckraking articles helped middle-class Americans get angry over the corruption of big business and politicians. They rallied public support for several new laws, including the Pure Food and Drug Act and the Hepburn Act (for railroad regulation) of 1906.

3 A muckraker can best be described as

  ① a sanitation worker
  ② an investigative reporter
  ③ a public relations manager
  ④ a farm employee
  ⑤ a political appointee

4 What was the reaction of the public to the work of the muckrakers?

  ① Their work was largely ignored by prosperous Americans.
  ② Citizens vocally supported local industry and commerce.
  ③ Voters were displeased with President Roosevelt.
  ④ Readers rejected their writing as too disgusting.
  ⑤ People were angry and demanded new legislation.

Summarizing the Main Idea

Summarizing the main idea in social studies materials is finding the key thought. When you read a newspaper article, you will often find the key thought in the headline.

After reading the following paragraph, think about what you would most likely see as a headline for the passage.

> Charles Lindbergh, piloting the Spirit of St. Louis, has landed at Le Bourget Field in Paris. He has completed the first-ever transatlantic flight. He touched down 33 hours and 30 minutes after taking off from Roosevelt Field on Long Island, New York. Encountering fog and sleet, he had to fly blind part of the way at an altitude of 1,500 feet. At times he flew only 10 feet above the waves. His flight covered a distance of 3,610 miles. Since he was flying solo and his plane had only one engine and no radio, he had very little room for error. Lindbergh is getting a hero's welcome in Paris.

Your headline should be similar to "Lindbergh Completes First Transatlantic Flight." The headline in *The New York Times* on May 22, 1927 was, "Lindbergh Does It!"

The **topic** of a passage is what that passage is about. The **main idea** is what the passage is trying to say about the topic.

Reading Selection

In 1859, while prospecting in Colorado, George Griffith discovered gold. He called his claim George's Town. The next year, word of his discovery spread and the valley swarmed with other treasure seekers. But no more gold was found. Instead, other men discovered silver in the nearby mountains a few miles away in a place that came to be called Silver Plume. For the next decade, George's Town—or Georgetown, as it later came to be known—was the greatest silver producer in the world.

1 Given the information in the reading selection, how would you summarize its main idea?

_____

Test Taking Tip

Main idea GED questions usually have an incorrect choice that is too broad to be the main idea and at least one choice that is too narrow to be the main idea and just focuses on one detail.

GED Practice

Question 1 refers to the following passage.

Citizens of the United States, it is clear, have a great many rights that give them freedoms all peoples hold dear: the freedom to think what they like; to voice those opinions, individually to their elected representatives or collectively in small or large assemblies; to worship as they choose or not to worship at all; to be safe from unreasonable searches of their persons, their homes, or their private papers. However, the theory of democratic government holds that along with these rights come responsibilities: to obey the laws; to pay legally imposed taxes; to serve on juries when called to do so; to be informed about issues and candidates; and to exercise the right to vote that has been won for so many through the toil and tears of their predecessors.

—"Responsibilities of Citizenship"
by Alonzo L. Hamby

1 The key thought of the passage is

  ① Citizens have a great many rights and freedoms.
  ② Citizens have the freedom to think what they like.
  ③ Citizens have a responsibility to obey the laws.
  ④ Citizens have both rights and responsibilities.
  ⑤ Citizens should value the right to vote, which others fought for.

Question 2 refers to the following passage.

The Sumerians created the world's earliest civilization in the southern part of what is now called Iraq around 3000 B.C. They were responsible for important inventions such as large-scale irrigation, the first wheeled vehicles, and the potter's wheel. They are credited with inventing writing, and with it, history, mathematics, astronomy, and law. Their city-states, such as Ur and Uruk, are considered the first cities. Their clay tablets contain the world's oldest examples of record keeping and literature.

2 What is the main idea of this passage?

  ① Many aspects of modern life first appeared in ancient times.
  ② The Sumerian civilization began around 3000 B.C.
  ③ The Sumerians created many of the foundations of civilized life.
  ④ History began with the invention of writing by the Sumerians.
  ⑤ People today should appreciate the contributions of the Sumerians.

Question 3 refers to the following passage.

In the United States, every person and institution is subject to the rule of law. The legislative branch of our government, Congress, passes laws. The executive branch of the government, which includes the president, carries out the laws. The judicial branch, the courts, applies and interprets the laws. This distribution of responsibilities, known as the separation of powers, protects the freedom of Americans.

3 What is the main idea of this passage?

  ① Political power should not be concentrated in any one person.
  ② Political power in the United States is shared among three branches.
  ③ Every person and institution is subject to the rule of law.
  ④ The judicial branch is responsible for justice in the United States.
  ⑤ The separation of powers helps protect the freedom of Americans.

Identifying Implications

Implications are ideas that are suggested, or implied, but not stated directly. When a writer implies an idea, he or she usually gives clues. As a reader, you need to pick up on and understand the clues in order to make an accurate conclusion.

When you read the following paragraph, think about what the writer is implying about British motivations in China in the nineteenth century.

> In this era of the War on Drugs, it is hard to imagine a Western democracy actively promoting drug addiction. Yet that is exactly what happened during the Opium Wars between the United Kingdom and China. British traders had been illegally exporting opium to China. The resulting widespread addiction was causing serious social and economic disruption in the country. In 1839, the Chinese government confiscated all opium stored in Canton by British merchants. Within days, the British had provoked a military conflict and won a quick victory. They demanded and were given special trade and residence rights. In 1856, a second Opium War, with France joining the United Kingdom, was fought. It resulted in the importation of opium into China being legalized along with other humiliating Chinese trade and power concessions.

The writer is implying that the United Kingdom was willing to do almost anything to promote its economic and political power in China. It went to war to protect the property of British merchants. With its victory it won special trade, residence and control rights. In other words, the British motivation was not a desire to spread drug use. That was just a way for it to get what it really cared about, increased economic and political power.

Figuring out the writer's implications is often called "reading between the lines."

Reading Selection

The Cold War was a period of East-West competition, tension, and conflict short of full-scale war. During that time, the two military-political alliances accused each other of hostile intention. After World War II, there were disputes between the Soviet Union and the Western democracies. The Soviet takeover of East European states led Winston Churchill to warn in 1946 that an "iron curtain" was descending through the middle of Europe. During the Cold War there were real wars that happened. They were called "proxy wars" because the USSR and the U.S. never directly fought against each other. For example, in Vietnam, the U.S. fought the Viet Cong, not the USSR. In Afghanistan, the USSR fought the mujahideen, not the U.S. There was also competition for influence in the Third World and a major superpower arms race.

1 Who does the writer imply was responsible for the Cold War?

_____

2 What was Winston Churchill implying when he warned of an "iron curtain" descending through the middle of Europe?

_____

GED Practice

Questions 1 and 2 refer to the following passage.

Manifest Destiny was a term used by leaders and politicians in the 1840s to explain continental expansion by the United States. The people of the United States felt it was their mission to extend the "boundaries of freedom" to others. They wanted to share their idealism and belief in democratic institutions with people who were perceived as being incapable of self-government, such as Native Americans and those of non-European origin.

But there were other forces and political agendas at work as well. As the population of the original 13 colonies grew and the U.S. economy developed, the desire to expand into new land increased. For many colonists, land represented potential income, wealth, self-sufficiency, and freedom. Expansion into the western frontiers offered opportunities for self-advancement.

1 Which of the following statements about the 1840s can be inferred from the passage?

  ① Americans were sensitive to the Native American cultures of the West.

  ② Americans were threatened by the growth of an independent Mexico.

  ③ Manifest Destiny was a sham meant to be a cover for American greed.

  ④ Americans were justified in their mistreatment of the Native Americans.

  ⑤ Pioneers were mainly motivated by their desire to live better.

2 Which of the following beliefs from the 1840s have been discredited?

  ① Democracy is a form of government that appeals to many people.

  ② Native Americans are incapable of democratic self-government.

  ③ The United States should promote freedom throughout the world.

  ④ Individuals should have the opportunity to improve their lives.

  ⑤ Economic development helps the United States prosper.

Questions 3 and 4 refer to the following passage.

Relatively unknown outside his own state, Warren Harding was a true "dark horse" presidential candidate. He won the 1920 Republican Party nomination due to the political scheming of his friends after the nominating convention could not pick a nominee. Before receiving the nomination, Harding was asked whether there were any embarrassing episodes in his past that might be used against him. His formal education was limited, he had a long-standing affair with the wife of an old friend, and he was a social drinker. But Harding answered "no," and the party moved to nominate him. Only after the nomination did Harding tell them of his affair with Carrie Fulton Phillips. By then, it was too late to find another nominee. To reduce the likelihood of a scandal breaking, the Republican National Committee sent Carrie and her family on a trip to Japan and paid them over $50,000. Mrs. Phillips also received monthly payments thereafter, becoming the first and only person known to have successfully extorted money from a political party.

3 What can the reader infer about Carrie Fulton Phillips?

  ① She believed deeply in family values.

  ② She worked hard to provide her family with a special vacation.

  ③ She loved Warren Harding and wanted to help him succeed.

  ④ She was a skilled political fundraiser for the Republicans.

  ⑤ She was willing to exploit others for her own personal gain.

4 What most likely would have been the reaction if Harding's affair had become public?

  ① It would have been ignored.

  ② It would have caused an uproar and cost Harding votes.

  ③ It would have created a backlash of sympathy for Harding.

  ④ It would have made Carrie Fulton Phillips very popular.

  ⑤ It would have helped Carrie Fulton Phillips's career.

Applying Given Ideas

Sometimes you need to show your understanding of what you read by taking information from a passage and **applying** it to another situation. On the GED exam, you might be given information such as an amendment to the Constitution. You might then be asked to identify which choice is a correct application of that amendment.

> The Monroe Doctrine states that the United States will not permit any European nation to extend its holdings or use armed force on the two American continents.

Which of the following would be considered a challenge to the Monroe Doctrine?
- In 1962, the Soviet Union sends ballistic missiles to Cuba, just 90 miles from the U.S.
- In 1994, mobs in Mogadishu, Somalia, attack American soldiers from downed helicopters.
- In 2005, Hugo Chavez, president of Venezuela, criticizes the U.S. at the United Nations.

Only the first example would be considered a challenge to the Monroe Doctrine since the USSR was a European nation trying to introduce armed forces in Cuba. Cuba is an island off of North America and is covered by the Monroe Doctrine.

Somalia is in Africa, which is not covered by the Monroe Doctrine.

Hugo Chavez is the president of a Latin American country. He is not from Europe.

> A progressive tax is a tax that is most costly to wealthy people. A regressive tax is a tax that is most costly to poorer people.

Rate the following four taxes from 1 to 4, where 1 is the most progressive tax and 4 is the most regressive tax.

A graduated income tax, where higher income levels are taxed at   _____
higher rates.

A state lottery to support education, where purchasers are hoping   _____
to strike it rich.

A property tax, which is based on the value of a person's home.   _____

An inheritance tax, where estates over $10 million are taxed   _____
50 percent.

Special GED Item Type

One way the GED Social Studies Test will test your ability to apply given ideas is to use an item similar to the one below. Five categories are defined and then the questions present a situation. You will need to select which of the five categories would apply to the situation presented.

Below are some major points of five of the ten amendments to the Constitution that make up the Bill of Rights.

Amendment 1: Freedom of religion is guaranteed. Freedom of speech and freedom of the press are guaranteed.

Amendment 2: Because an armed militia is necessary for the security of a free state, people have the right to keep and bear arms.

Amendment 4: People have the right to be secure in their persons, houses, papers, and effects so they are protected against unreasonable searches and seizures. No warrants shall be issued, but upon probable cause, and describing the place to be searched, and the persons or things to be seized.

Amendment 5: No person shall be subject for the same offense to be twice put in jeopardy of life or limb. Nor shall a person be compelled in any criminal case to be a witness against himself. A person may not be deprived of life, liberty, or property, without due process of law.

Amendment 6: In all criminal prosecutions, the accused shall enjoy the right to a speedy and public trial, by an impartial jury, and to be informed of the nature and cause of the accusation; to be confronted with the witnesses against him; to have the chance to obtain witnesses in his favor, and to have a lawyer for his defense.

For each of the following situations, select which amendment would apply. Then state your reason why that amendment applies.

1 O.J. Simpson was found innocent of the murder of his wife, Nicole. Months later, new evidence was discovered that indicated that he might have been guilty of the crime.

_____

2 Citing the War on Terror as justification, the Bush administration has claimed the right to detain suspects without bringing charges. Some of these suspects have been held at the Guantanamo Bay base in Cuba for years.

_____

3 A Native American tribe has petitioned the court for permission to use peyote in its religious ceremonies. Peyote is a powerful natural drug that has been used in the tribe's ceremonies for centuries.

_____

GED Practice

Questions 1–3 refer to the following information.

Every country in the world has some form of government. Below are the most common forms of government.

Monarchy—Rule of a single person who is the permanent hereditary head of state.

Dictatorship—Rule of a single person who rules by threat of force.

Feudalism—Local power holders are granted land and, in return, provide military help to the ruler.

Representative democracy—People elect their representatives and government.

Theocracy—Rule by religious leaders who claim to be directed by God.

1 In Iran, even though there is an elected government, real power lies with the Shiite Islamic clerics led by Ayotollah Khamenei. This type of government is best described as a

　① monarchy
　② dictatorship
　③ feudalism
　④ representative democracy
　⑤ theocracy

2 In North Korea, Kim Jong Il has total power. Even during periods of starvation, the people have remained docile and obedient.

　① monarchy
　② dictatorship
　③ feudalism
　④ representative democracy
　⑤ theocracy

3 In South Africa, the African National Congress won the last election. They have won every election since the end of apartheid.

　① monarchy
　② dictatorship
　③ feudalism
　④ representative democracy
　⑤ theocracy

Question 4 refers to the following passage.

The 1951 Convention Relating to the Status of Refugees says that in order to qualify as a refugee, a person must:

- be outside his own country
- have "a well-founded fear of being persecuted" for one of a given set of reasons
- be "unable or, owing to such fear . . . unwilling to avail himself of the protection" of his country of origin

4 Which of the following people would qualify as a refugee?

　① an opposition political leader in Zimbabwe who has received death threats
　② a twelve-year-old boy now in the U.S. from Pakistan who fled forced factory work
　③ a middle-aged man in Germany who was tortured in Turkey before escaping
　④ a young woman in France who has fled a famine in Ethiopia
　⑤ a graduate student from Nigeria who is studying economics in the U.S.

Questions 5–7 refer to the following information.

Colonies in the Americas were founded by Europeans for a variety of reasons. They include:

Religious freedom—Colonists were leaving religious persecution in Europe.

Economic wealth—Colonial powers or individuals wanted the riches of a colony.

Civil order—Colonial powers sent their criminals to the colony.

Security—A new settlement was established to protect older settlements.

Missionary work—The colonists' major objective was to spread Christianity to Native Americans.

5 The Spanish conquistador Cortez conquered and destroyed the Aztec civilization in Mexico. He brought a fortune in gold back to Spain. What was his main reason for colonizing Mexico?

(1) religious freedom
(2) economic wealth
(3) civil order
(4) security
(5) missionary work

6 The Pilgrims settled in Massachusetts so that they could practice their religion freely. What was their main reason for coming to Massachusetts?

(1) religious freedom
(2) economic wealth
(3) civil order
(4) security
(5) missionary work

7 By 1675, Franciscan priests had settled in Hopi pueblos in New Mexico. They built churches and tried to convert the Hopis to Christianity. What was their main reason for being with the Hopis?

(1) religious freedom
(2) economic wealth
(3) civil order
(4) security
(5) missionary work

Question 8 refers to the following passage.

The Normans, led by William the Conqueror, invaded Britain in 1066. They became the rulers of Britain. However, within a few generations, they had assimilated. They became more British than Norman.

8 Which of the following is most similar to the description of assimilation of a conqueror by the conquered described above?

(1) The grandson of Mongol invader Genghis Khan, Kublai Khan, adopted the Chinese way of life.
(2) British conquerors of India kept their customs even though they were vastly outnumbered by the native Indian population.
(3) Germanic invaders of northern Europe wiped out ancient Roman culture and created a feudal society.
(4) Pioneers from the United States that settled Texas revolted from Mexican rule and created an independent republic.
(5) Polynesians spread their culture across the previously uninhabited islands of the Pacific.

Applying Remembered Ideas

In the last chapter, you practiced applying ideas and facts from reading passages to different situations. On the GED, you will also need to apply knowledge you have gained from prior learning or experience, rather than from information in a passage.

> A headline in early 2006 stated "Stock Market reaches highest level since 9/11."

The newspaper assumed that the reader knew that 9/11 referred to the terrorist attacks of September 11, 2001. On that day, airplanes flown by terrorists destroyed the twin towers of the World Trade Center in New York City and damaged the Pentagon in Washington, D.C. The newspaper also assumed that the reader knew that 9/11 was a great turning point in American history.

On the GED, you will be expected to **apply prior knowledge** of events, people, and ideas to new situations. In some cases, you may not know about the person, place, or event. This does not mean that you cannot pass the GED Social Studies test. It does mean that you should try to learn about key events and ideas of American and world history. Reading newspapers and magazines, as well as listening to or watching the news, can also help. If you are aware of current events, it will help you figure out some answers, even if you don't know all of the details.

Reading Selection

One of the great environmental disasters in American history was the Dust Bowl of the 1930s. The southwestern Great Plains had been used for grazing livestock. But in the 1920s, millions of acres were plowed for wheat farming. The area usually had only 20 inches of rain a year, which is barely enough for farming. In the early 1930s, there was a severe drought. With the deep-rooted native grasses gone, there was nothing to hold the soil. As a result, there were great dust storms. Thousands of families were forced to leave the region, which did not recover for years.

1 Can you think of an environmental disaster that occurred in the early twenty-first century that had an impact similar to the Dust Bowl?

_____

_____

2 How was that disaster similar to the Dust Bowl and how was it different?

_____

_____

GED Practice

Question 1 refers to the following information.

The Code of Hammurabi is the oldest known document of laws; it dates from 1750 B.C. It was discovered on a pillar in Susa, which was once a large city in what is now Iran. It contained laws for the Babylonian Empire. The laws include economic provisions (prices, tariffs, trade, and commerce) and family law (marriage and divorce), as well as criminal law (assault, theft) and civil law (slavery, debt).

1 Which of the following important American documents is most similar to the Code of Hammurabi?

   ① the Mayflower Compact
   ② the Declaration of Independence
   ③ the United States Constitution
   ④ the Emancipation Proclamation
   ⑤ the "I Have a Dream" Speech

Question 2 refers to the following information.

Every year, thousands of people from Africa and Asia try to enter Europe by boat. If they are successful, they land unnoticed on beaches in Spain and Italy. Unfortunately, many of them are caught by authorities, and others die in shipwrecks or at sea. Even if they are able to escape detection and capture, they face more challenges. Since they lack identification papers, they cannot work legally. That makes them subject to exploitation in the underground economy. They often lack medical care and have no legal protection.

2 Which group is most like the Africans and Asians described in the passage?

   ① illegal immigrants from Mexico
   ② tourists from Japan
   ③ graduate students from China
   ④ Native Americans leaving a reservation
   ⑤ African Americans moving north

Question 3 refers to the following passage.

Varanasi is one of the holiest cities in India. It is located on the banks of the Ganges River. Every year, over one million Hindu pilgrims come to Varanasi. The city is surrounded by a road known as Panchakosi; every devout Hindu hopes to walk this road and visit the city once in a lifetime. They also want to bathe in the Ganges River.

3 Which of the following cities is most similar to Varanasi?

   ① New York City, the site of the Columbus Day parade
   ② Rio de Janeiro, the location of the Carnival celebration
   ③ Mecca, the destination of the hajj, a pilgrimage that is a Pillar of Islam
   ④ Washington, D.C., capital of the United States
   ⑤ Memphis, where fans go to Graceland, home of Elvis

Question 4 refers to the following information.

In 1959, the Dalai Lama, the spiritual head of Tibetan Buddhism, fled Tibet along with many of his followers. Today, Tibet is controlled by China. Many Chinese people have followed the Dalai Lama and moved from Tibet. The Dalai Lama and his Tibetan followers have been facing the challenge of keeping their religion alive while they have been banished from their homeland.

4 Which of the following groups faced a similar situation to what the Dalai Lama and his followers face today?

   ① the Irish after they were driven out of Ireland by the Potato Famine
   ② the South Vietnamese who fled with U.S. troops at the end of the Vietnam War
   ③ Brigham Young and the Mormons who relocated to Utah
   ④ the Jewish people after they were driven out of Jerusalem by the Romans
   ⑤ the Roman people who left India and settled throughout Europe

6

Distinguishing Facts from Opinions and Hypotheses

Look at the following statements:

> 1. The United States and its allies defeated the Axis powers of Germany, Japan, and Italy in World War II.
>
> 2. The American soldiers who won World War II should be known and remembered as the greatest generation.
>
> 3. Soldiers fighting for freedom have an advantage against soldiers fighting for conquest.

The first statement is a **fact.** It can be proved to be true. The Allies did defeat the Axis powers in World War II.

The second statement is an **opinion.** An opinion is a statement about the writer's feelings or ideas about a topic. Often, an opinion cannot be completely proved or disproved. While the writer believes the American soldiers of World War II are the greatest generation, an argument could also be made that other generations might be greater.

The third statement is a **hypothesis.** A hypothesis is a possible explanation that can be tested. Hypotheses can be proved or disproved. In this case, coming up with a case in which an army of conquest destroyed an army fighting for freedom would be evidence against the hypothesis.

Reading Selection

(1) In 2000, the states with the greatest number of immigrants were California, Texas, New York, and Florida. (2) These states are extremely fortunate to have so many residents from other countries. (3) States with large immigrant populations are more likely to have a growing economy than states with a small number of immigrants. (4) Many immigrants pay taxes. (5) They will often work in the least desirable and lowest paying jobs. (6) As more people become aware of the contributions of immigrants, the United States will become more welcoming of them. (7) And the sooner that happens, the better.

On the lines in next to each sentence number, write *F, O,* or *H.* You will write *F* if you think the sentence is a fact. You will write *O* if you think the sentence is an opinion. You will write *H* if you think the sentence is a hypothesis.

1 _____   5 _____

2 _____   6 _____

3 _____   7 _____

4 _____

GED Practice

Questions 1 and 2 refer to the following passage.

The Renaissance was a period of great social, political, and intellectual change in Europe. While Italy was the center of the Renaissance, the rest of Europe was also involved.

Instead of completely depending on the authority of the church, Renaissance thinkers depended on rational thought. Art and architecture applied this new thinking. Artists such as Michelangelo, da Vinci, and Raphael created great works of art that expressed their new understandings of perspective and proportion.

The development of cities and a new middle class in Europe helped fuel changes in the economy. Better ships were developed. These ships allowed European adventurers to explore Africa and Asia, and to discover the Americas. By the sixteenth century, the advances of the Renaissance had made Europe a better place to live.

1 Which of the following is an opinion expressed by the author?

(1) The Renaissance was a period of great social, political, and intellectual change in Europe.

(2) While Italy was the center of the Renaissance, the rest of Europe was also involved.

(3) Artists such as Michelangelo, da Vinci, and Raphael created great works of art.

(4) The development of cities and a middle class in Europe helped fuel changes in the economy.

(5) By 1500, the advances of the Renaissance had made Europe a better place to live.

2 Which of the following is a hypothesis of what caused the Renaissance?

(1) Depending on rational thought rather than authority led to the Renaissance.

(2) The term *renaissance* means "rebirth" and refers to a period of great change.

(3) The artists, inventors, and thinkers of the Renaissance are remembered today.

(4) The discovery of the Americas was the greatest achievement of the Renaissance.

(5) The Renaissance is one of the most important periods in world history.

Question 3 refers to the following passage.

In 1981, a gunman tried to kill President Reagan. Reagan was slightly wounded, but his press secretary, James Brady, was paralyzed by his gunshot wound. As a result of his injury, he and his wife Sarah Brady campaigned for a new gun control law that became known as the Brady Bill.

For over a decade, they campaigned for their bill. Finally, in February 1993, Congress considered the Brady Bill. It was referred to the House Judiciary Committee, which then sent the bill to a subcommittee. The Subcommittee on Crime and Criminal Justice held a hearing in September, 1993, and sent the bill back to the full committee the next month. In November, the Judiciary Committee supported the bill and the Rules Committee scheduled a debate on the House floor. The House passed the bill on November 10 and sent it to the Senate, which passed the bill ten days later with an amendment.

Since the House and Senate bills were now different, a conference was scheduled to agree on one bill. Just three days later, the conference had agreed on one bill and the House of Representatives voted to support that bill. The next day, the Senate approved the bill by a voice vote and sent it to the White House. On November 30, 1993, President Clinton signed the bill, and it became law.

In the United States, new laws are created in Congress. A bill is introduced in one of the two houses of Congress, the Senate or the House of Representatives. It usually will have one or more sponsors. The sponsor has to be a member of the Chamber of Congress that is considering the bill.

3 Which of the following is a fact about the Brady Bill?

(1) The process to pass the Brady Bill was too long and complicated.

(2) The Judiciary Committee did a good job working on the Brady Bill.

(3) The bill could have been defeated if the gun lobby wasn't overconfident.

(4) The Brady Bill became law 12 years after James Brady was shot.

(5) Without the Bradys' public relations effort, the bill would have failed.

Drawing Conclusions

The great fictional detective Sherlock Holmes examined clues to solve crimes. His examination of the evidence would lead him to a solution of the crime. He would draw conclusions based on the information he was given.

When you read GED Social Studies passages, you will be asked to **draw conclusions** based on the evidence that is given in a passage. Sometimes, you must also use your general knowledge and understanding of logic to draw a correct conclusion.

> In the 2006 parliamentary elections in Iraq, observers expected most voters to vote for the party representing their religious or ethnic group. Few people were expected to vote for secular parties attempting to represent the entire nation. Sunni Arabs make up about 20 percent of the Iraqi population. Kurds make up about 20 percent of the Iraqi population. Shiite Arabs make up about 60 percent of the Iraqi population.

Given the information in the above passage, who would you expect to win the parliamentary elections?

The information in the passage lets you draw the conclusion that a party representing the Shiites would be expected to win the election. The voters were expected to vote for their own religious or ethnic group. The Shiites are by far the largest group. Therefore, it is reasonable to conclude that the party representing Shiites would probably win.

Reading Selection

Thailand is the only nation in Southeast Asia that was never a colony of a European power. Its independence was in the most danger during the nineteenth century. Both the United Kingdom and France took territory from the kingdom, which was then called Siam. In 1855, King Mongkut signed a trade treaty with the British. In the next few years, he also signed trade treaties with other European powers and the United States. Rather than trying to isolate Siam from Western influence, the king started the modernization of his kingdom. He developed relationships with many Western nations, never becoming overly dependent on just one nation.

1. In the early nineteenth century, the Southeast Asian country of Vietnam allowed French missionaries into the country. A few years later, Vietnam tried to drive out the French and have no contact with the West. Given the information in the passage, what conclusion can you make about Vietnam's policy?

   _____

   _____

2. What was the evidence that helped you draw your conclusion?

   _____

   _____

GED Practice

Questions 1 and 2 refer to the following passage.

Many people believe that education can lead the way out of poverty and despair. Many Native American leaders living on reservations shared that belief. They believed that starting colleges on their reservations would help their people. The Navajo Nation established the first tribal college, Navajo Community College, in 1968. By 2006, there were more than 30 tribal colleges located on reservations in the United States. In addition to community colleges, they also include colleges and universities. Many of these institutions run on far less money than most American colleges and universities. They get support from the American Indian College Fund. The Bill and Melinda Gates Foundation also supports these colleges. Less support comes from successful Indian casinos than you might expect.

1 What is a conclusion that you can draw from this passage?

   (1) Tribal casinos provided the funding for the tribal colleges.
   (2) In ten years, there will be over 100 tribal colleges.
   (3) Native Americans are now prosperous and wealthy.
   (4) The colleges have improved conditions on the reservations.
   (5) The Navajo Nation is the most highly educated Native American tribe.

2 What is the most important evidence that education is helping Native Americans?

   (1) The colleges get financial support from the Bill and Melinda Gates Foundation.
   (2) The number of colleges has grown from one to over 30 in less than 40 years.
   (3) The first tribal college, Navajo Community College, was established in 1968.
   (4) The tribal colleges run on far less money than most American colleges.
   (5) It has been proven that education leads the way out of poverty and despair.

Question 3 refers to the following passage.

At the end of World War II, American leaders feared that widespread destruction, along with poverty and unemployment, would be fertile ground for the spread of communism in Europe. Americans wanted to create stability and prosperity in the region in order to promote the continuation and spread of democracies. In 1947, Secretary of State George C. Marshall presented a plan to rebuild European economies. The United States would pay for the plan, which became known as the Marshall Plan.

From 1948 to 1951, the United States sent $13 billion of economic aid to several European countries. The aid helped restore industry and agriculture, mostly by funding European companies. Trade expanded and the recipients thrived. By the end of the Marshall Plan, the participating nations of Europe were stable, growing, and committed to democracy.

3 What is a conclusion that could be drawn from this passage?

   (1) Helping countries to help themselves is an effective way of promoting peace and prosperity.
   (2) Military action is more effective than economic assistance in promoting democracy.
   (3) Once countries become dependent on assistance, they never learn to take care of themselves.
   (4) Economic assistance should require that all contracts to be given to American companies.
   (5) The Marshall Plan was a mistake because it made Europe a strong competitor of the United States.

Recognizing Persuasive Language

> Join the next American Revolution. Be one of the leaders. Get the best power and performance of any SUV on the market.

Have you seen ads like this one selling new SUVs? Advertisers want you to buy their product or service. Therefore, they will use language meant to **persuade** you to believe that you must have what they are selling.

What does the advertiser do to convince you to buy their SUV? The American Revolution means many things to Americans. If you "join the next American Revolution," the implication is that you are someone to be admired, a leader. Phrases like "best power and performance" are also meant to persuade.

Advertisers are not the only ones who try to persuade their audience. Politicians, newspaper columnists, and advocacy groups such as the Sierra Club and Focus on the Family try to influence public opinion.

Often, you will see very different opinions on the same issue. Writers will use emotionally charged words and images in an effort to influence you.

Reading Selection

In 2006, physician-assisted suicide was a hotly debated issue. Below are arguments for and against physician-assisted suicide. What does each writer do to try to convince you to support his or her position?

1. The right to a good death is a basic human freedom. There are many people dealing with unbearable pain while they suffer from an incurable terminal illness. They are being treated cruelly by those who would deny them any possibility of relief.

_____

_____

2. We want to build a culture of life. We need to value human life at all stages. It is immoral to allow a person to end their own life. That will only lead to a culture of death. This will lead to depressed people being encouraged to kill themselves by greedy relatives eager to get their wealth.

_____

_____

GED Practice

Question 1 refers to the following passage.

The proposed constitution for the European Union (EU) would create a "superstate" that would end the independence of the individual member nations. The EU has developed the institutions, powers, mechanisms, behaviors, and habits of a state. But it has done this without the active participation of its people. As it is written, the proposed constitution will give too much power to the political elite based in Brussels, the headquarters of the EU. It has been created, developed, and extended by unelected politicians, with a minimum of popular participation.

1 The writer of this passage would probably want the reader to support all of the following ideas except to

  (1) support and vote for the EU constitution in its current form

  (2) insist that all EU member nations keep their identities

  (3) involve the people of European nations in discussions of reforms

  (4) work to make a new constitution that will serve the people better

  (5) have each EU member nation continue to control its foreign policy

Question 2 refers to the following passage.

You don't have to wait for the government to act in order to save a lot of energy. You can start by using compact fluorescent lightbulbs in your home. If you must own a vehicle, a sporty hybrid gas-electric car uses much less energy than a gas-guzzling SUV. Sleep better at night by turning down your thermostat. Planting shade trees and bushes, especially on the south and west sides of your house, can cut air-conditioning needs. If you are able to do all of these things, you should proudly think of yourself as a protector of the planet.

2 The writer of this passage would most likely want to persuade the reader to

  (1) go to their neighborhood church and pray on a regular basis

  (2) try to only buy products made in the United States

  (3) vote for the candidate of their choice on Election Day

  (4) use warm or cold water instead of hot to clean clothes

  (5) support the charity of their choice with contributions

Question 3 refers to the following passage.

In 2006, Robert Mugabe was president of Zimbabwe, a nation in Africa.

You can count on anyone with the courage to oppose British and American interests to be attacked by the press. If you stand up for your country, you are painted as a devil. If you are willing to sell out your country to international bankers and the United States, then you are an angel. It's clear that London and Washington decided long ago that it was time for our beloved president, Robert Mugabe, to go. His program of true land reform, his independence and leadership, and his distrust of neo-colonial economics have turned him into an outsider. Their plan is simple: buy the opposition, fund anti-Mugabe organizations and media, threaten sanctions, and accuse Mugabe of electoral fraud.

3 What picture of Robert Mugabe would the writer want you to believe?

  (1) He is a ruthless dictator who will do anything to stay in power.

  (2) He has failed to manage his relationship with the United States.

  (3) He is a patriot defending his nation from foreign control.

  (4) He is trying to crush his opposition and silence the media.

  (5) He is trying to bring election reform to Zimbabwe.

Recognizing Unstated Assumptions

> Rock Hudson became one of the world's most popular film stars in the 1950s. He was tall, dark, and handsome, and he perfectly fit the public's image of a romantic, masculine hero. In 1985, he told the press that he had AIDS. He was a famous, wealthy Republican who had been a symbol of heterosexuality. The public was shocked.

Why do you think that the public was shocked? Many people assumed that anyone who looked like Rock Hudson and was a romantic film star had to be heterosexual. But Rock Hudson was gay.

Writers often make **unstated assumptions** in their work. Sometimes those assumptions are well-founded, but sometimes they are not.

As a reader, you need to be on the lookout for unstated assumptions.

Reading Selection

In 2003, the American government accused Saddam Hussein of making weapons of mass destruction. They also accused the Iraqi government of having links to terrorists.

After American military forces invaded Iraq, they were unable to find weapons of mass destruction. However, President Bush still assured the nation that attacking Iraq was a crucial part of the War on Terrorism. He claimed that if we did not confront the terrorists in Iraq, we would have to fight them in the United States.

1. What was an unstated assumption of President Bush when he claimed that if we did not confront the terrorists in Iraq, we would have to fight them in the United States?

_____

_____

GED Practice

Question 1 refers to the following passage.

In 1415, King Henry V invaded France with an army of 11,000 men. In two months, he had lost half his army to battle and disease. A much larger French army of about 30,000 men confronted Henry's army at Agincourt. Most of the French were heavily armed knights, while most of the British were archers. Surprisingly, Henry's army won a great victory at Agincourt.

1 Why would it be surprising that the army of Henry V won at Agincourt?

(1) An English army defeated a French army.

(2) An army of archers defeated an army of knights.

(3) A smaller army defeated a much larger army.

(4) An experienced army defeated an inexperienced one.

(5) A well-led army defeated a poorly led one.

Question 2 refers to the following passage.

In 1938, the Sudetenland was part of Czechoslovakia. It was also home to over 3 million Germans. Adolph Hitler demanded that the Sudetenland become part of Germany. The British and the French had treaties to defend Czechoslovakia. The prime minister of Great Britain, Neville Chamberlain, wanted to avoid war at all costs. He met with Hitler and the French premier, Édouard Daladier. They agreed that the German Army would take over the Sudetenland. Chamberlain returned home to welcoming crowds who were relieved that the threat of war had passed. Chamberlain told the British public that he had achieved "peace in our time."

2 What assumption did Neville Chamberlain make?

(1) If Hitler felt threatened by the British, he would cooperate.

(2) If Hitler was given what he wanted, he would be satisfied.

(3) The British public was supportive of Hitler's ambitions.

(4) The Czechs did not deserve the protection of the British.

(5) Germans in the Sudetenland had the right to rejoin Germany.

Question 3 refers to the following passage.

The right to vote is one of our most important rights. When we vote, we help decide who will govern us. However, many Americans do not vote. They say it does not matter who is elected. Or sometimes, it is just too difficult to make it to the polls. What they often don't realize is that even though their vote is secret, it is a public record whether or not they voted. If they don't vote, they lose no matter who wins.

3 What is an assumption that the writer is making?

(1) Voting does not matter because politicians lie.

(2) People have good reasons for not voting.

(3) If people planned better, they would vote.

(4) Politicians fix elections in order to win.

(5) Politicians treat voters better than nonvoters.

Question 4 refers to the following passage.

During the Cold War, the United States and the Soviet Union had hundreds of missiles pointed at each other. Each missile carried nuclear bombs capable of destroying entire cities. Yet none of these weapons were ever used. Both sides understood that a nuclear strike would result in nuclear retaliation. Policy makers called this mutual assured destruction (MAD). The best way to ensure peace was to produce so many powerful weapons that they could not be destroyed. Investing in thousands of nuclear weapons would lead to a tense but stable peace.

4 Mutual assured destruction depends on all of the following assumptions except

(1) Nuclear powers will act rationally in their self-interest.

(2) Nuclear weapons will be delivered by traceable missiles.

(3) All leaders care about the survival and health of their citizens.

(4) A rogue general would never be able to launch a nuclear missile.

(5) Nuclear states might collapse and lose control of their weapons.

10 Identifying Cause and Effect Relationships

Maytag has closed its Galesburg, Illinois manufacturing plant. The closing has resulted in 1,600 workers losing their jobs. Those jobs will now be moved to factories in Mexico. The impact of this closing will be devastating: including lost jobs at nearby suppliers to indirect effects of declining consumption and reduced tax revenues, the total job loss in the region will be over 4,100. With a population of about 34,000, Galesburg will be hard-hit by this change. Unemployment is up and those laid-off workers who have found new jobs are making far less than they were before.

This passage describes a **cause and effect relationship**. One event results in other things happening. The cause is Maytag closing its plant. One effect is many workers losing their jobs and having to live with far less income. Another effect is many other businesses in the Galesburg area being hurt by this change.

Reading Selection

Sometimes you will read a passage in which one cause has many effects. Throughout history, there are many examples of the opposite situation. Many causes can contribute to one effect.

The American Revolution began in April, 1775, when Americans fought British soldiers at the Battles of Lexington and Concord in Massachusetts. Many actions and decisions helped cause this momentous event. A decade earlier, the French and Indian War cost the British a great deal of money. They looked to taxing the American colonies to raise money. First they tried to enforce the Navigation Acts. Throughout the colonies, the Navigation Acts were not obeyed. The British decided to send an army of 10,000 men to the colonies. They decided to pay for the army through a Stamp Tax on the colonies. The opposition was so widespread that the British repealed the Stamp Tax, but insisted on keeping a tax on tea. The colonists boycotted the tea. In Boston, the Sons of Liberty boarded ships carrying the tea and dumped the tea in the harbor. We remember that incident today as the Boston Tea Party. In retaliation, the British sent more forces and occupied Boston. They expected the colonists to back down when they saw the British forces. Instead, the colonists increased their preparations to confront the British. When the British attempted to capture the American leaders John Hancock and Sam Adams at Lexington, the American minutemen were ready for them. A revolution was about to begin.

❶ What were some of the causes of the American Revolution?

_____

_____

❷ Were there any common themes that you see among the many individual causes of the Revolution?

_____

_____

GED Practice

Question 1 refers to the following passage.

The Great Depression of the 1930s was the worst economic slump in U.S. history. While the depression began with the stock market crash of October, 1929, the causes of the depression began much earlier. One of the main causes for the Great Depression was the greatly unequal distribution of wealth throughout the 1920s. The government worked to increase the concentration of wealth by dramatically cutting federal income taxes and inheritance taxes for the rich. Wealth was concentrated in just a few industries, especially automobiles and radio. At the international level, the United States was wealthy while Europe was unable to fully recover from World War I. This imbalance of wealth created an unstable national and world economy. Confidence was the only thing keeping the system going. With the stock market crash, confidence was replaced with fear. Many of the rich lost their fortunes. Items bought on credit had to be returned. As the economy collapsed, people stopped spending and businesses closed. The Great Depression quickly spread around the world.

1 All of the following are causes of the Great Depression except

   ① the stock market crash of 1929
   ② the unequal distribution of wealth
   ③ high income and inheritance taxes
   ④ wealth concentrated in a few industries
   ⑤ confidence being replaced by fear

Question 2 refers to the following passage.

The law of supply and demand is one of the foundations of economics. It states that the price of a good or service will be stable when there is a balance between the amount of the item available and the number of items that would be sold at a given price. If the price of an item is too high, not all of the items will be sold. This will exert pressure to reduce the price. If the price of an item is too low, then all the items will sell and people will ask for more.

2 What would be the expected effect of more toaster ovens being produced than can be sold?

   ① The toaster ovens would have to be redesigned.
   ② The price of toaster ovens would go down.
   ③ Customers would prefer to buy other products.
   ④ There would be an increase in the cost of toasters.
   ⑤ The production of toaster ovens would increase.

Question 3 refers to the following passage.

In the 1980s, the Central Intelligence Agency (CIA) worked with Pakistan to create the Taliban. A Marxist government ruled in Afghanistan and Soviet troops occupied the country. The U.S. provided $3 billion for building up Islamic groups in Afghanistan.

Madrassas, or radical Muslim theological schools, were established on the Pakistan side of the border. Young Afghan refugees were recruited to fight the Soviets. The Soviets withdrew from Afghanistan and the Taliban moved swiftly to take over.

The United States was now seen as an enemy of Islam. The Taliban provided a safe haven for Al-Qaeda, a terrorist organization whose mostly Arab members had also fought against the Soviets. The CIA was right in concluding that the Islamic fundamentalists would be the most effective fighters against the Soviets. They did not anticipate that they would develop into dangerous enemies of the United States.

3 All of the following were effects of the Soviet occupation of Afghanistan except

   ① the CIA encouraged radical Islamic groups to come to Afghanistan
   ② the Afghan fighters were very effective against the Soviet forces
   ③ madrassas were established on the Pakistani side of the border
   ④ the Afghan fighters were grateful for the help they got from the CIA
   ⑤ the Taliban established a radical Islamic fundamentalist government

Recognizing the Writer's Point of View

> Thar's three hundred dead Yankees buried here under our feet. I helped to put 'em thar, but so help me God, I hope the like'll never be done in this country again. Slavery's gone and the war's over now, thank God for both! We are all brothers once more, and I can feel for them layin' down thar just the same as fur our own.

Who do you think was the speaker in the above passage? The references to Yankees and slavery places the time of the passage around the Civil War. When the speaker says, "I helped to put 'em thar," he identifies himself as a Confederate soldier.

Whenever you read, you should try to figure out the **point of view** of the writer. First person accounts can take place in a time and place different from our own.

Reading Selection

We left Boston this morning at about 8 o'clock for Albany, by way of the Western Railroad.

After shaking hands and bidding such of our friends as had gathered at the station a good-bye, we seated ourselves in the cars, and as they began to move, the spectators that had gathered in and around the station sent up three most hearty cheers for the California adventurers; and they were very readily and heartily returned by us, while we were started on our way with railroad speed toward the land of gold.

We had a special car into which no intruder was allowed to trespass, and I believe a more jolly company of men has seldom been found. We arrived at Springfield, Mass., at about noon where we were fortunate in procuring a fine dinner, to which all did ample justice. After we had eaten we were soon on our way again.

We arrived at Greenbush, N.Y., before night, where we had some little trouble with the baggage master about procuring our trunks, which had been checked at Boston, as we had failed to procure the corresponding checks. However, after some little dispute he gave them up and we took the ferry boat for Albany on the opposite side of the Hudson.
—Excerpted from *California As I Saw It: First-Person Narratives of California's Early Years, 1849–1900* by Kimball Webster

❶ What time period is the writer describing? What clues did you use to figure out the time period?

_____

_____

❷ Where were the writer and his companions going and what did they expect was going to happen?

_____

_____

GED Practice

Questions 1 and 2 refer to the following passage.

Sunday afternoon August 18, nineteen planes with propellers turning, lined up at Clover Field, Santa Monica, California. Will Rogers was on the loud speaker to point out the humorous aspects of such an event. Taking their cue from him, newspaper men coined descriptive names for the affair before contestants reached their first stop. It was generally called the "powder puff derby" and those who flew in it variously as "Ladybirds," "Angels" or "Sweethearts of the Air." (We are still trying to get ourselves called just "pilots.")

Finishing a race, as in anything else, is as important as starting, and sixteen of the women crossed the white line at the end. This was the highest per cent of "finishers" in any cross country derby, up to that time, for men or women.

—Excerpted from *The Fun of It, Random Records of My Own Flying and of Women in Aviation* by Amelia Earhart

1 The writer of this account is most likely

   ① a pioneering woman pilot
   ② comedian Will Rogers
   ③ a newspaper reporter
   ④ a top woman athlete
   ⑤ a typical woman of her time

2 When did the event described in this passage probably take place?

   ① during the 1780s at the time of the American Revolution
   ② at the beginning of the Industrial Revolution around 1820
   ③ at the beginning of the era of flight shortly after 1900
   ④ between the two World Wars during the late 1920s
   ⑤ during the beginning of the women's movement in the 1970s

Questions 3 and 4 refer to the following passage.

A month later, on Saturday, June 17, the FBI night supervisor called Felt at home. Five men in business suits, pockets stuffed with $100 bills, and carrying eavesdropping and photographic equipment, had been arrested inside the Democrats' national headquarters at the Watergate office building about 2:30 A.M.

By 8:30 A.M. Felt was in his office at the FBI, seeking more details. About the same time, *The Post*'s city editor woke me at home and asked me to come in to cover an unusual burglary. . . .

This was the moment when a source or friend in the investigative agencies of government is invaluable. I called Felt at the FBI, reaching him through his secretary. It would be our first talk about Watergate. He reminded me how he disliked phone calls at the office but said the Watergate burglary case was going to "heat up" for reasons he could not explain. He then hung up abruptly.

I was tentatively assigned to write the next day's Watergate bugging story, but I was not sure I had anything . . . I picked up the phone and dialed 456-1414—the White House—and asked for Howard Hunt. . . . I reached Hunt and asked why his name was in the address book of two of the Watergate burglars.

"Good God!" Hunt shouted before slamming down the phone.

—Excerpted from "How Mark Felt Became 'Deep Throat'" by Bob Woodward

3 The person who wrote this passage is most likely

   ① a supporter of the Democratic Party
   ② an employee of the FBI
   ③ a paid Washington lobbyist
   ④ an expert in security systems
   ⑤ a newspaper reporter

4 The writer of this passage was probably most interested in

   ① linking the crime to the president
   ② seeing the burglars in prison
   ③ getting the true and accurate story
   ④ protecting his friends from suspicion
   ⑤ becoming famous for his articles

Recognizing the Historical Context of a Text

Look at the following passage and try to decide when it might have been written and by whom.

> Although the vast country which we have been describing was inhabited by many indigenous tribes, it may justly be said at the time of its discovery by Europeans to have formed one great desert. The Indians occupied without possessing it. It is by agricultural labor that man appropriates the soil, and the early inhabitants of North America lived by the produce of the chase. Their implacable prejudices, their uncontrolled passions, their vices, and still more perhaps their savage virtues, consigned them to inevitable destruction.
>
> —Excerpted from *Democracy in America* by Alexis de Tocqueville

The passage is from *Democracy in America*, written by Alexis de Tocqueville in the 1830s. His view of Native Americans contains inaccuracies, as well as generalizations about their character.

Reading Selection

Widely dispersed over the great land mass of the Americas, they numbered approximately 75 million people by the time Columbus came, perhaps 25 million in North America. Responding to the different environments of soil and climate, they developed hundreds of different tribal cultures, perhaps two thousand different languages. They perfected the art of agriculture, and figured out how to grow maize (corn), which cannot grow by itself and must be planted, cultivated, fertilized, harvested, husked, and shelled. They ingeniously developed a variety of other vegetables and fruits, as well as peanuts and chocolate and tobacco and rubber.

—Excerpted from *A People's History of the United States* by Howard Zinn

❶ How are these two passages alike?

_____

_____

❷ What are the important differences between the two passages?

_____

_____

❸ When do you think the second passage might have been written?

_____

Hint: As you read Social Studies materials, try to figure out the time and place that the passage was written and the time and place that is being described.

Questions 1 and 2 refer to the following passage.

On the topmost tower there is a spacious temple, and inside the temple stands a couch of unusual size, richly adorned, with a golden table by its side.

Below, in the same precinct, there is a second temple, in which is a sitting figure of Jupiter [Marduk], all of gold. Before the figure stands a large golden table, and the throne whereon it sits, and the base on which the throne is placed, are likewise of gold. The Chaldaeans told me that all the gold together was eight hundred talents' weight. In the time of Cyrus there was likewise in this temple a figure of a man, twelve cubits high, entirely of solid gold. I myself did not see this figure, but I relate what the Chaldaeans report concerning it. Darius, the son of Hystaspes, plotted to carry the statue off, but had not the hardihood to lay his hands upon it. Xerxes, however, the son of Darius, killed the priest who forbade him to move the statue, and took it away. Besides the ornaments which I have mentioned, there are a large number of private offerings in this holy precinct.

—Excerpted from *The Histories* by Herodotus

1 Which of the following is most likely the time and place of this description?

  ① the city of Babylon in the Middle East around 450 B.C.
  ② a northern European town in 1000 during feudal times
  ③ a Shinto shrine in medieval Japan in 1200
  ④ the Papal States in Italy during the Renaissance in 1500
  ⑤ a museum exhibit in a large American city 50 years ago

2 What description of the writer's would not be believed as true today?

  ① The temples contained an enormous amount of gold.
  ② The god chose the native woman who stayed in his temple.
  ③ The Chaldaeans, the priests, told him about the temples.
  ④ Darius, king of Persia, was too superstitious to take a gold statue.
  ⑤ Xerxes had a priest killed in order to take away a solid gold statue.

Questions 3 and 4 refer to the following passage.

I did not meet Miss Adams until 1900, so in turning back to tell her story before then, I must call upon what others have said, upon her papers, and upon what she has, most fortunately, written about herself. . . .

Miss Adams's grandfather, Barnabas Lothrop Adams, who was born in Canada, found his way to Iowa, where he married Julia Ann Banker. There they fell in with Brigham Young and his Mormons, became converts, and joined them in their long trek through the wilderness in search of a haven. That was in 1847, while the country in which they finally settled was still owned by Mexico. Asenath Ann Adams, Miss Adams's mother, was born about three weeks after the Mormons ended their wild and dangerous journey.

Brigham Young set his people to building a town, and to tilling the wastelands. Not the least of his concerns was to erect a theatre, for which he and his elders would choose the plays. Mr. Walter Prichard Eaton says it "was in its day the most remarkable playhouse in America. Remarkable first because it was built at all," long before any railroad reached Utah.

— Excerpted from *Maude Adams: An Intimate Portrait* by Phyllis Robbins

3 The person who wrote this passage most likely

  ① was a Mormon pioneer
  ② lived in the early twentieth century
  ③ was critical of the theatre
  ④ was a relative of Miss Adams
  ⑤ was a newspaper reporter

4 Which of the following statements is not supported by the passage?

  ① While a young man, Barnabas Adams left his family to travel west.
  ② Asenath Ann Adams was one of the first Mormons born in Utah.
  ③ Three generations of Miss Adams's family were Mormons.
  ④ The Mormons disapproved of having a theatre in Salt Lake City.
  ⑤ Brigham Young was the leader of the Mormons in Utah.

Identifying Comparisons and Contrasts

On the GED, you will be asked to read a passage and then identify how two things **compare** or **contrast**. For example, read this passage about two economic systems. How are the two systems alike? How are they different?

> In a capitalist economy, people are allowed to have private property. The money they earn can be spent on goods and services with few restrictions. Most of the means of creating wealth, such as factories and businesses, are privately owned. People have the opportunity to accumulate great wealth, but also run the risk of not having enough to survive.
>
> In a Communist economy, all property belongs to the state. Many goods and services are rationed by the state based on need. The means of creating wealth are owned by the state. The state controls many aspects of private life.

You have to search to find any similarities between these two systems. In both systems, there are factories and businesses. Both systems try to address the needs of their people. But how they operate is entirely different. A capitalist economy, by putting property in the hands of individuals, gives them the power and responsibility to manage their economic life. There is a chance of great reward, but also the chance for disaster. A Communist economy puts all resources in the hands of the government in an attempt to be fair and equitable.

In reality, few economies are either purely Communist or purely capitalist. In even the most capitalist countries, the government is very important in managing the economy. In addition, countries with an officially Communist economy allow many capitalist practices.

Reading Selection

The twentieth century will be remembered as a period of great brutality. People from very different races and cultures engaged in genocide, the intentional attempt to destroy a culture or ethnic group. The Turks were guilty of murdering over one million Armenians early in the century. The German Nazis killed over six million Jews in the Holocaust. Joseph Stalin was responsible for the murder of millions in the Soviet Union. The Khmer Rouge murdered over a million Cambodians while trying to destroy their culture and history. And in Rwanda, radical Hutus murdered over 800,000 Tutsis.

1 How were these different racial and ethnic groups alike?

_____

_____

2 How were these different racial and ethnic groups different?

_____

_____

GED Practice

Question 1 refers to the following passage.

While the twentieth century might be remembered as the American century, the twenty-first century might be the Asian century. The two most populous nations on Earth, China and India, currently have the two most rapidly growing economies on Earth. The two Asian nations are providing the entire world with goods and services in many areas from textiles to computers. The two nations also have the two most rapidly increasing standards of living in the world. While both nations still have many millions of desperately poor citizens, they have the most rapidly growing middle classes in the world.

But their governments are very different. India is the world's most populous democracy. It has had free elections for over half a century. After many years of one-party rule by the Congress Party, it is now a multi-party democracy. Elections are contested and are mostly free and fair. Since 1949, the People's Republic of China has been ruled by the Communist Party. The party has always tried to control many aspects of Chinese citizens' lives, including their thoughts. The Chinese now are trying to promote economic freedom and progress while continuing to severely restrict political freedom.

1. India and China are similar in all the following ways except

    (1) they have more residents than any other nation
    (2) they have rapidly growing economies
    (3) they have many very poor citizens
    (4) their citizens have a choice in elections
    (5) they have a growing middle class

Question 2 refers to the following passage.

The first two presidential elections of the twenty-first century were among the closest in American history. Americans were nearly evenly divided between Republicans and Democrats. With only a few exceptions, the states and regions voted the same way in both elections. On Election Day, all the networks broadcasted maps of the United States to show who won which state. They all colored Republican states red and Democratic states blue. As a result, many people called states that voted Republican "red states" and states that voted Democratic "blue states."

Blue states tended to be on the coasts and in the upper Midwest. They tended to be the old industrial heartland of the United States. They also were the most cosmopolitan states. The people in those states tended to be more secular and liberal. Red states dominated the South and West. They tended to be rural and conservative. Many people in the red states identified themselves as fundamentalist Christians.

2. Red and blue states are different in every way except

    (1) the dominant religious beliefs in the state
    (2) consistency in the way they voted for president
    (3) the political views of a majority of their citizens
    (4) the concentration of older factories in the state
    (5) the regions of the country in which they are located

Judging Information

During a trial, the jury often hears a very different account of events from the prosecution and the defense. After hearing all the evidence and listening to all the witnesses, the jury needs to come to a verdict. They have to evaluate everything they saw and heard. They have to **judge** all the information presented to them and decide which version of events is closer to the truth.

When you read, you also have to judge the information you read. You can compare what you are reading with your own experience. You can also think about whether or not what you are reading is consistent and makes sense.

Just like a trial has standards of evidence, you as a reader need to have criteria to judge the truth of what you are reading.

> Segregation is an issue of states' rights. The federal government is overstepping its bounds when it declares that a state must desegregate its schools, its transportation, or its businesses. This is a case of an arrogant, powerful central government imposing its will on the law-abiding people of our state.
>
> The federal courts have no regard for the general welfare of our institutions. They are not hesitating to impose the harshness of the full force of the U.S. government on the people of our sovereign state. Every state has the right to decide on its own whether or not to desegregate.

1 The above arguments were made by many southerners during the 1950s and 1960s as they tried to stop desegregation. What do you think might be some flaws in their argument?

_____

_____

_____

GED Practice

Question 1 refers to the following passage.

In general, Americans believe that democracy can solve many of the problems of the world. We believe that people want to live in peace. If given the chance, people will elect governments that will want to get along with their neighbors. They will choose governments that will make their lives better.

❶ Which of the following is not evidence supporting the above theory?

  ① Canadian and American democracies have been allies for many years.

  ② Under the dictatorship of Mussolini, Italy conquered Ethiopia.

  ③ Palestinians elected Hamas, a party that wants to destroy its neighbor Israel.

  ④ Most of the democracies of Europe have voluntarily joined the European Union.

  ⑤ The democratically elected government of Nigeria sent peacekeepers to Liberia.

Question 2 refers to the following passage.

The law of supply and demand is a theory that explains how prices are set. In general, the theory states that the price of an item is the point at which supply equals demand. In other words, when the price of an item is raised, the theory predicts that fewer customers would want to purchase that item. If the price is lowered, more customers would want to purchase the item.

❷ Which of the following does not support the theory of supply and demand?

  ① When Macy's put all men's suits on sale for 30 percent off, sales increased.

  ② Customers pay more for the same item at Lord & Taylor than at Sears.

  ③ One hundred dollar tickets for the Super Bowl can be scalped or resold for $500.

  ④ As more companies built more computers, their price dropped.

  ⑤ As the number of stamp collectors has dropped, so has the price of most stamps.

Question 3 refers to the following passage.

For many years, international development concentrated on expensive, high profile projects in the developing world. In general, these projects were a disappointment. They had many negative unintended consequences and did not improve the economy of the developing nation. In recent years, a different approach has been gaining popularity. The theory is that projects that are proportional to the current state of a nation's economy have a greater chance of success. Projects are most effective when they concentrate on delivering benefits to a major segment of the population of a nation, rather than to a few foreign investors. Projects that are dedicated to sustainable development, which helps the economy without hurting the environment, are most likely to succeed.

❸ Which evidence does not support the above passage?

  ① The 1970 Aswan High Dam, the greatest source of electricity for Egypt, powers the economy.

  ② Microloans to women in Bangladesh have helped them become independent.

  ③ Brazilian road building into the Amazon has led to widespread destruction of the rain forest.

  ④ Many large factories that were built throughout Africa in the 1970s are now abandoned.

  ⑤ Through ecotourism, Costa Rica has improved its economy and protected the environment.

Recognizing Values

Mohandas Gandhi did not become the political and spiritual leader of the Indian people by promising them great wealth and power. Instead, he taught them to stand up for their rights through nonviolent protest. Rather than inflicting suffering on his enemies, he encouraged his followers to willingly accept suffering themselves.

His powerful method of ending injustice was called *sātyagraha,* or devotion to truth. He insisted on resisting the adversary without rancor and fighting him without violence. He first developed *satyagraha* while helping the Indian community in South Africa fight discrimination. He later used it in India to help his nation achieve independence from the United Kingdom.

From this passage, we can see that Gandhi lived by his **values** including deep beliefs in justice and nonviolence. His main adversaries were the British. They were vulnerable to his tactics because they also had a belief in justice.

Reading Selection

At the Council of Clermont in 1095, Pope Urban II preached for a Crusade to the Holy Land. He also promoted the Truce of God, which called for an end to wars between the nobles of Europe and the end to widespread banditry. While it might seem odd that the same council promoted war and peace, the link was that a motivation for the Crusade was the idea of giving aid to fellow Christians in the East. The Crusaders also believed that war to defend Christian society was a holy work that served God. Protecting pilgrimages to Jerusalem was an important motive for the Crusaders. They responded in unexpected numbers to the call to secure Jerusalem for Christians.

❶ What were some of the values that motivated the first Crusaders?

_____

_____

_____

GED Practice

Questions 1, 2, and 3 refer to the following definitions.

Multiculturalism–respect and reverence for the uniqueness of all cultures

Nationalism–loyalty and devotion to the nation-state is more important than other individual or group interests

Human Rights–rights that belong to an individual or group of individuals as a consequence of being human

Justice–treating individuals and groups fairly and equitably

Morality–observing customary standards of right and wrong

1 The following section of the Declaration of Independence is based upon which value?

We hold these truths to be self-evident, that all men are created equal, that they are endowed by their Creator with certain unalienable Rights, that among these are Life, Liberty and the pursuit of Happiness.

  ① multiculturalism
  ② nationalism
  ③ human rights
  ④ justice
  ⑤ morality

2 The National Museum of the American Indian is now open in the Mall in Washington, D.C. It attempts to represent all the native cultures of the Americas. When creating an exhibit, it strives to get input from the American Indian groups that will be represented. The National Museum of the American Indian promotes which value?

  ① multiculturalism
  ② nationalism
  ③ human rights
  ④ justice
  ⑤ morality

3 One of the first violent clashes leading up to the American Revolution was the Boston Massacre. An unruly mob threatened a small group of British soldiers, who shot into the crowd, killing five people. They were tried for murder. A leader of the movement for independence, John Adams, agreed to be the defense lawyer for the British soldiers despite his hostility towards the British government. In this case, John Adams was primarily motivated by what value?

  ① multiculturalism
  ② nationalism
  ③ human rights
  ④ justice
  ⑤ morality

Judging the Adequacy of Facts

For a person to be convicted of a crime in a criminal court, the jury must believe the suspect is guilty beyond a reasonable doubt. They must decide that the facts of the case are **adequate**, or enough for them to reach a conclusion of guilt. Otherwise, they must find the defendant innocent.

When you read, you must decide whether or not there are sufficient facts presented to justify the conclusions of the writer.

A patent is a government grant of the exclusive right to make, use, or sell an invention for a number of years. A patent can be granted either for a new product or an important improvement of another product. Patents can be granted for machines, industrial or agricultural products, and the processes needed to make them. For a patent to be valid, the invention must be different and useful. It needs to be an important development. In addition, it cannot be just an obvious change from an existing product.

Reading Selection

A company has applied for a patent for a new type of peanut butter and jelly sandwich. Instead of using two slices of bread, the sandwich uses a pita pocket. The pita has a slit going one-third of the way around its circumference. Using the slit, the peanut butter and jelly can be placed inside the pita and spread with a knife.

1 Given the explanation of what a patent is, and the description of the new peanut butter and jelly sandwich, explain what information is needed to determine whether or not the new sandwich should be patented.

_____

_____

_____

2 Look at the criteria for granting a patent and the description of the new peanut butter and jelly sandwich. Should the company be granted the patent? Explain how you arrived at your decision.

_____

_____

_____

GED Practice

Question 1 refers to the following passage.

The first commercial oil well was drilled in Titusville, Pennsylvania in 1859. In 1870, John D. Rockefeller founded Standard Oil Company. Using dishonest and unfair methods, he controlled most of the oil produced in the United States by 1900. Control of the oil industry allowed Rockefeller to amass a great fortune estimated at over one billion dollars at its peak.

In 1911, the United States Supreme Court determined that Standard Oil was a monopoly and ordered it to be broken up into independent companies. Rockefeller became one of the world's great philanthropists by setting up four major charitable organizations and donating over five hundred million dollars.

1 Which of the following statements is not adequately supported by facts from the passage?

  ① Pennsylvania was the first place in the world to have an oil industry.

  ② John D. Rockefeller used dishonest and unfair methods to create a monopoly.

  ③ John D. Rockefeller was able to amass a fortune of over one billion dollars.

  ④ The Standard Oil Company was broken up because it was a monopoly.

  ⑤ John D. Rockefeller was one of the great philanthropists of his time.

Question 2 refers to the following speech given by President Johnson.

Why are we in South Vietnam?

We are there because we have a promise to keep. Since 1954 every American President has offered support to the people of South Viet-Nam. We have helped to build, and we have helped to defend. Thus, over many years, we have made a national pledge to help South Viet-Nam defend its independence. And I intend to keep that promise. . . .

We are also there to strengthen world order. Around the globe, from Berlin to Thailand, are people whose well being rests, in part, on the belief that they can count on us if they are attacked. To leave Viet-Nam to its fate would shake the confidence of all these people in the value of an American commitment and in the value of America's word. The result would be increased unrest and instability, and even wider war.

We are also there because there are great stakes in the balance. Let no one think for a moment that retreat from Viet-Nam would bring an end to conflict. The battle would be renewed in one country and then another. The central lesson of our time is that the appetite of aggression is never satisfied.

—Excerpted from a speech given by President Johnson at Johns Hopkins University, April 7, 1965

2 Which of the following statements is not supported by the information provided in the passage?

  ① President Johnson was not the first American president to defend South Vietnam.

  ② When the United States makes a pledge, it never backs down from its word.

  ③ Countries around the world depend on the United States to defend them.

  ④ Leaving South Vietnam would ruin people's faith in America.

  ⑤ A retreat from Vietnam would lead to wars in other countries.

Comparing and Contrasting Different Viewpoints

Have you ever watched election coverage on television? Just before the polls close, the campaign manager of each candidate is interviewed. He or she claims that things are going well. Since only one candidate in a race will win, one of the campaign managers is not being accurate. He or she is either misreading the situation or trying to put a happy face on a grim turn of events.

We have become accustomed to this example of "spin." We expect these partisans to look at events in the most favorable light possible. As an objective observer, it is your job to compare what each person is saying. You then need to check it against any outside information you might have. This will help you determine which person is giving a more accurate picture of what is really going on.

When reading, you also have to be able to **compare and contrast different viewpoints** and evaluate them for accuracy.

Reading Selection

For many years, historians had a very negative view of the nomads of Asia. Surviving manuscripts described them as vicious barbarians. They were seen as cruel and savage. It was thought they had no hint of compassion or humanity. Part of the problem with this picture is that the nomads were not literate. As a result, all of the written accounts were by the people they were attacking. The writers from the agricultural and urban societies being invaded condemned the invaders. As a result, the Scythians, the Huns, the Visigoths, and the Mongols are remembered as fierce and ruthless destroyers.

If we look at the effect of barbarian conquests on the civilizations they conquered, a more complex picture emerges. After each of these groups conquered existing civilizations, they tended to mix with the conquered. They would intermarry with the local population and live among them. Often what resulted was a combination of the best qualities of the nomads, including their resourcefulness, courage, and toughness, with the best qualities of the conquered civilization. When the ancient Sumerians were conquered by nomadic Semites, the new empires of Akkad and later Babylonia created new and more powerful civilizations. When the Mongols conquered China, it was China that became revitalized. And when the Vikings, invading by sea instead of by land, conquered England and northern France, these two areas became the sites of two of the most powerful and dynamic kingdoms of an emerging Europe.

① If the ancient nomads had been literate, what kind of accounts might they have written of their conquests? How would they differ from the accounts we have today?

_____

_____

_____

GED Practice

Questions 1 and 2 refer to the following excerpts.

Excerpt from the National Party submission:

This was the situation that confronted young members of the National Party at the beginning of the 'sixties. The issues that we debated deep into the night centered on the question of how we could come to grips with this changing world on the one hand, and yet retain our right to our own national self-determination on the other? How would we avoid the chaos that was sweeping much of the rest of Africa—that was depicted in horrific photographs of refugees fleeing from the Congo or Angola—and yet ensure justice and full political rights for Black South Africans? How could we defend ourselves against expansionist international communism and terrorism and yet make all South Africans free?

The solution that we then came up with was "separate development."

We thought that we could solve the complex problems that confronted us by giving each of the ten distinguishable Black South African nations self-government and independence within the core areas that they had traditionally occupied. In this way we would create a commonwealth of South African states—each independent, but all co-operating on a confederal basis with one another within an economic common market.

Excerpt from the African National Congress submission:

During the 1960s, concurrent with the creation of the new "security state" and new legislation, the apartheid rulers embarked on radical new forms of social engineering designed to defend and entrench white minority rule, which had far-reaching consequences. A social order already distinctive for deep-seated, legalized inequalities premised upon racial classification now experienced new levels of what has been characterized in authoritarian societies as "bureaucratic terrorism." In essence, bureaucratic terror in South Africa involved the use of state power against individuals and groups who are already economically subordinate, socially discriminated against, and politically without rights. Instances of the phenomenon included:

- huge numbers of arrests (in the 1960s hundreds of thousands annually) for contravention of pass laws;
- large-scale forced removals and resettlements, mainly to the Bantustans;
- the clearance of so-called "black spots" (pockets of land held in freehold by African farming communities);
- the endorsing out of urban areas of so-called "surplus people";
- the redefinition of all Africans as "citizens" of ethnic homelands or Bantustans.

The implementation of basic apartheid measures meant that basic "first generation" human rights—such as the franchise, civil equality, freedom of movement or association—were denied systematically and massively.

—Excerpted from the South African Truth and Reconciliation Commission

1 The National Party most likely represented which group in South Africa?

  ① young adults who were interested in social justice

  ② the Afrikaners, descendents of white Dutch settlers

  ③ the Zulus, the most powerful tribe of black Africans

  ④ black militants fighting for equal rights and freedoms

  ⑤ white racists who wanted to kill black Africans

2 The African National Congress most likely represented which group in South Africa?

  ① young adults who were interested in social justice

  ② the Afrikaners, descendents of white Dutch settlers

  ③ the Zulus, the most powerful tribe of black Africans

  ④ black militants fighting for equal rights and freedoms

  ⑤ white racists who wanted to kill black Africans

Identifying Faulty Reasoning

The source of a great deal of prejudice and hate in the world is **faulty reasoning**.

> The terrorists who hijacked the airplanes on 9/11 were all Arab. Therefore, all Arabs are terrorists.

This reasoning is obviously false. It is faulty reasoning to generalize from a few individual cases to an entire ethnic or cultural group. Yet we encounter this kind of reasoning often. A newspaper runs a story about a welfare cheat. An impression is left that all people on public assistance are cheats. A Congressman is sentenced to jail for taking bribes. Some people then conclude that all Congressmen take bribes. When you read, you need to be on the lookout for faulty reasoning.

Reading Selection

On December 7, 1941, the Japanese attacked Pearl Harbor. The United States declared war against Japan and its allies, Germany and Italy. Lieutenant General John L. DeWitt, head of the Western Defense Command, was in charge of the defense of the Pacific Coast. "In the war in which we are now engaged," he wrote (Secretary of War) Stimson on February 14 (1942), "racial affinities are not severed by migration. The Japanese race is an enemy race, and while many second- and third-generation Japanese born on United States soil, possessed of United States citizenship, have become 'Americanized,' the racial strains are undiluted. . . . It therefore follows that along the vital Pacific Coast over 112,000 potential enemies of Japanese extraction are at large today." "A Jap's a Jap," he proclaimed later, "and that's all there is to it."

❶ What are the errors of logic and examples of prejudice expressed by DeWitt?

_____

_____

_____

❷ If you were studying racism in the United States, what questions would the above passage raise?

_____

_____

_____

GED Practice

Question 1 refers to the following passage.

President George W. Bush justified invading Iraq by claiming that it had weapons of mass destruction. Saddam Hussein, the brutal dictator of Iraq, had a record of oppressing his people, using poison gas on the battlefield and against unarmed civilians, and invading his neighbors. However, after the United States occupied Iraq, weapons of mass destruction were never found.

1 Which of the following is not a reason many Americans believed that Iraq had weapons of mass destruction?

  ① Americans wanted to believe and trust their president.
  ② Iraq had used poison gas, a weapon of mass destruction.
  ③ Saddam Hussein had a past record of secret weapons programs.
  ④ President Bush had a record of never distorting the truth.
  ⑤ Iraq had a history of threatening and attacking its neighbors.

Question 2 refers to the following passage.

The Cherokees, [who lived in the Southeast U.S.] in 1828 were not nomadic savages. In fact, they had assimilated many European-style customs, including the wearing of gowns by Cherokee women. They built roads, schools and churches, had a system of representational government, and were farmers and cattle ranchers. A Cherokee alphabet, the "Talking Leaves" was perfected by Sequoyah.

In 1830 the Congress of the United States passed the "Indian Removal Act." Although many Americans were against the act, most notably Tennessee Congressman Davy Crockett, it passed anyway. President Jackson quickly signed the bill into law. The Cherokees attempted to fight removal legally by challenging the removal laws in the Supreme Court and by establishing an independent Cherokee Nation.

The Supreme Court led by Chief Justice John Marshall ruled that the Cherokee Nation was sovereign, making the removal laws invalid. The Cherokee would have to agree to removal in a treaty. The treaty then would have to be ratified by the Senate.

By 1835 the Cherokee were divided and despondent. Most supported Principal Chief John Ross, who fought the encroachment of whites starting with the 1832 land lottery. However, a minority (less than 500 out of 17,000 Cherokee in North Georgia) followed Major Ridge, his son John, and Elias Boudinot, who advocated removal. The Treaty of New Echota, signed by Ridge and members of the Treaty Party in 1835, gave Jackson the legal document he needed to remove the First Americans. Ratification of the treaty by the United States Senate sealed the fate of the Cherokee.

—Excerpted from "Trail of Tears" by Golden Ink

2 What was the most important failure of logic in the decision to remove the Cherokee from the southeast United States?

  ① They had developed an advanced culture, economy, and government.
  ② Congress passed a law authorizing the removal of Indians.
  ③ The Cherokee nation was a sovereign and independent nation.
  ④ The signer of the treaty, Ridge, did not represent the Cherokee.
  ⑤ The United States Senate quickly ratified the treaty.

Restating Map Information

Many of the skills you use when you read text you also need when you read maps. When you **restate information** from a map, you are taking visual information and restating it in words.

Look at the following map. It shows the path traveled by General Sherman's army in 1864 and 1865. How could you state in words the key information contained in this map?

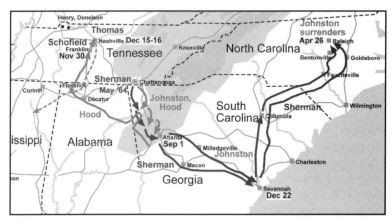

You could look at the details and say that Sherman's army marched through Georgia, South Carolina, and North Carolina in 1864 and 1865. Or you could say that Sherman's army marched through the heart of the South in 1864 and 1865.

The next series of maps show the growth of urbanization in the Las Vegas area from 1907 to 1995.

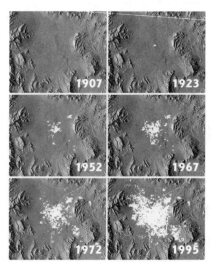

1. Restate in words the key information shown in this series of maps.

_____

_____

GED Practice

Question 1 refers to the following map.

SPANISH EXPLORATION OF NORTH AMERICA

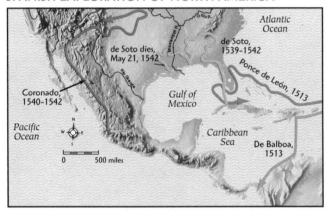

1 According to the information in this map

   ① Ponce de León explored the Great Lakes
   ② Coronado was the only explorer to cover the West
   ③ De Soto brought Christianity to large areas of North America
   ④ De Balboa had the largest group of explorers traveling with him
   ⑤ Coronado explored the Mississippi River

Question 2 refers to the following map.

THE SILK ROUTES

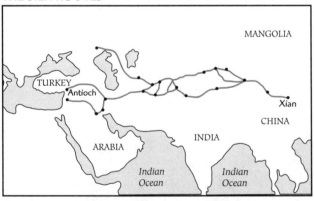

2 The map shows that the Silk Road was

   ① a paved road
   ② a major source of revenue
   ③ a trade route that linked China to the Middle East
   ④ a target for Central Asian nomadic armies
   ⑤ a busy highway between Xian and Antioch

Question 3 refers to the following map.

THE ARAB MUSLIM EMPIRE, 750 A.D.

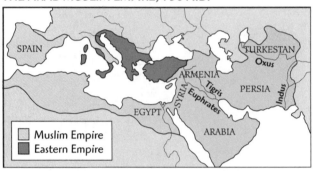

   ☐ Muslim Empire
   ■ Eastern Empire

3 All of the following information can be found on this map except

   ① in 750, the Arab Muslim Empire was the most powerful empire in the world
   ② the Arab Muslim Empire stretched from Spain to past the Indus River
   ③ the Arab Muslim Empire conquered the formerly Christian areas of Armenia and Spain
   ④ by 750, the Arab Muslim Empire was larger than the Eastern Empire
   ⑤ the Fertile Crescent, from Egypt to the valley of the Tigris, was under Muslim control

Identifying Implications

A map may contain **implications** beyond what is directly stated or illustrated.

Look at the map on the right of languages spoken in North America before 1763. What is one implication you can draw from this map?

The map shows that three different languages were spoken in what is now the United States. An implication you can draw is that it was a challenge to communicate in areas that spoke two or three different languages. You also might notice that most people spoke French. An implication of that fact is that French speakers were the largest and most powerful group.

NORTH AMERICA PRIOR TO 1763

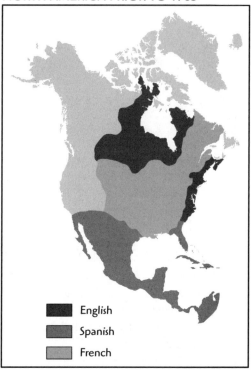

	English
	Spanish
	French

The next map shows the area around the North Pole, including the Arctic Ice Sheet.

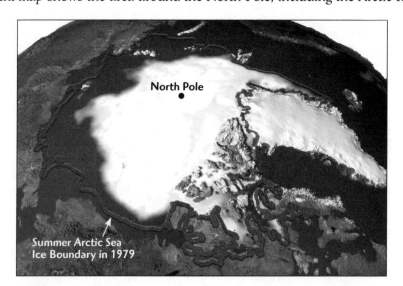

North Pole

Summer Arctic Sea
Ice Boundary in 1979

❶ What might be an implication of this map?

_____

_____

GED Practice

Question 1 refers to the following map.

1990 LIFE EXPECTANCY

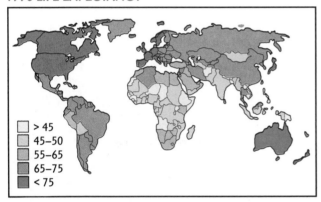

> 45
45–50
55–65
65–75
< 75

1 What is an implication you can draw about the United States, Canada, most of western Europe, Japan, and Australia?

(1) They have the best climates in the world.
(2) They have the best health care in the world.
(3) They have the strongest armies in the world.
(4) They all have similar racial and ethnic groups.
(5) They all have medical insurance for all citizens.

Question 2 is based on the following map of railroads in the eastern United States in 1860.

RAILROADS IN THE EASTERN UNITED STATES, 1860

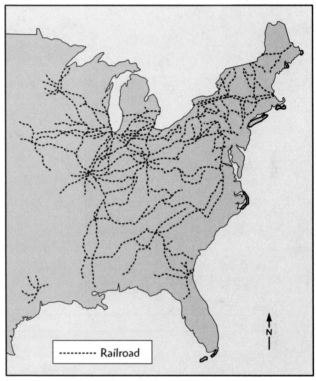

---------- Railroad

N

2 What is an implication you can draw from this map?

(1) People moved quickly by railroad rather than by car.
(2) The United States had the most extensive railroad system in the world.
(3) The North had a great transportation advantage over the South.
(4) The railroad lines were more of a financial burden in the North than they were in the South.
(5) More people lived in the South than the North.

Applying Map Information

Maps contain information that you can apply to make decisions. Hikers often use trail maps with contour lines. A **contour line** marks a certain elevation. If you hiked along a contour line, you would be hiking at a steady level. You would not be climbing or descending.

Look at the contour trail map on the left. Imagine you want to climb the highest peak. Can you find the highest elevation?

The highest elevation on the map is 6,612 feet. Notice that the contour lines are further apart at the highest elevations.

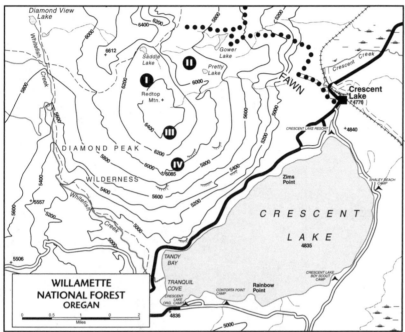

This is a road map of Colorado.

1 Imagine you are in Colorado Springs and you want to take the fastest route to Grand Junction. Using the map as your guide, describe the route you would take.

_____

_____

_____

_____

_____

_____

GED Practice

Question 1 refers to the following map.

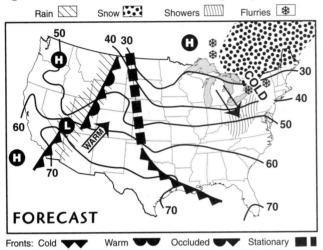

① You are about to leave on a vacation to Southern California. How should you pack?

  ① Bring winter coats, sweaters, wool shirts, and pants.

  ② Bring walking shoes and sweaters.

  ③ Bring raincoats, boots, and umbrellas.

  ④ Bring your swimsuit, sunglasses, and sunscreen.

  ⑤ Bring sweaters and cross-country skiis.

Questions 2 and 3 are based on the following map of home heating costs in the U.S.

HEATING YOUR HOME
Which Fuel Is Most Economical?

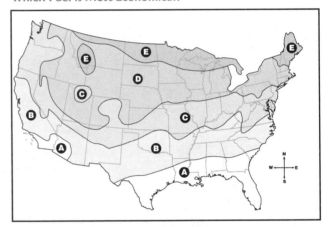

AVERAGE ANNUAL HOME HEATING COSTS WITH ALTERNATE FUELS

Fuel & Costs	Zone A	B	C	D	E
Oil	275	687	963	1155	1375
Gas	193	484	550	754	1001
Electricity	440	1089	1529	1848	2173
Wood	180	414	624	744	876

② What zone has the lowest heating costs in every fuel category?

  ① Zone A

  ② Zone B

  ③ Zone C

  ④ Zone D

  ⑤ Zone E

③ Katie and Tim live in upper New York State. How much do they spend a year to heat their home with gas?

  ① $754

  ② $1001

  ③ $550

  ④ $2173

  ⑤ $101

Identifying the Purpose and Use of a Map

Maps are tools that can be used for many purposes. Look at the following map of Superfund toxic waste sites in the United States. What do you think might be some uses for this map?

TOXIC WASTE SITES IN THE UNITED STATES

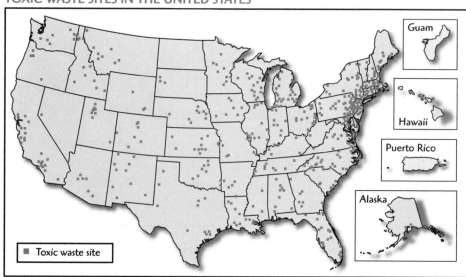

If you were an environmentalist, you might want to use this map to show that Superfund toxic waste sites are spread across the entire country. If you lived along the East Coast, you might be concerned about the concentration of Superfund sites and be more supportive of having the sites cleaned up. However, if you were looking for a place to live, you would probably want a more detailed map so that you would not buy or rent a home next to a Superfund site.

The following map shows Greek colonies from 750 B.C. to 500 B.C.

GREEK COLONIZATION c. 750–500 B.C.

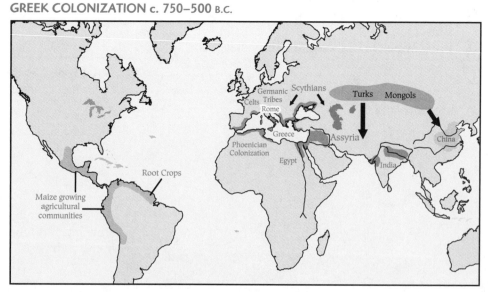

❶ What might be some possible uses for this map?

_____

_____

_____

GED Practice

Question 1 refers to the following map.

AVERAGE ANNUAL RAINFALL
in inches

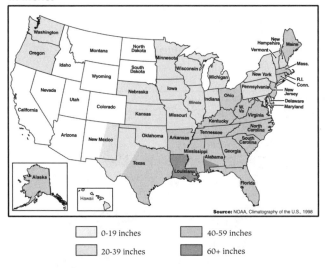

Source: NOAA, Climatography of the U.S., 1998

| | 0-19 inches | | 40-59 inches |
| | 20-39 inches | | 60+ inches |

1 Which of the following is a likely use for this map?

  ① planning water usage policies for every state
  ② predicting likely future industrial growth areas
  ③ citing dams and reservoirs for managing flood control
  ④ assigning water rights for various uses and localities
  ⑤ determining new routes for mass transit

Question 2 is based on the following map.

CENTERS OF ORIGINS OF FOOD PRODUCTION

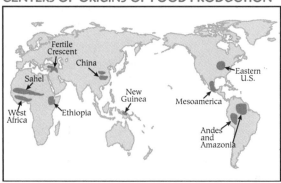

2 What is the most likely use for this map?

  ① determine the climate and resources needed for food production
  ② identify the nation with the largest population
  ③ identify which was the first origin of food production to appear
  ④ determine which cultures were the strongest
  ⑤ determine where the first civilizations developed

Identifying Comparisons and Contrasts

Maps can be powerful tools to illustrate **comparisons** and **contrasts**. Look at the following map. What areas of the world have the greatest urban growth? What continents have growth rates most similar to the United States?

The map shows that Asia, Africa, and Latin America have the greatest urban growth. Europe's growth rates are most similar to the United States. Neither of them have any large urban areas among the most rapidly growing.

URBAN POPULATION GROWTH (1995–2000)

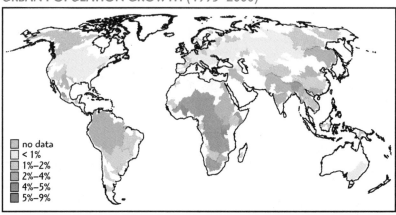

no data
< 1%
1%–2%
2%–4%
4%–5%
5%–9%

The following map shows per capita income by state in the United States in 1999.

UNITED STATES INCOME PER CAPITA BY STATE

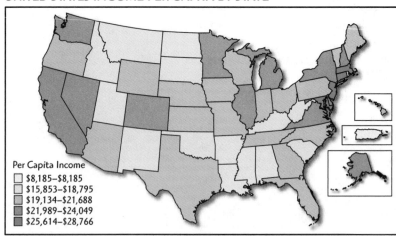

Per Capita Income
$8,185–$8,185
$15,853–$18,795
$19,134–$21,688
$21,989–$24,049
$25,614–$28,766

❶ Find your state and write its per capita income here: _____

❷ Find another state that has a similar per capita income: _____

❸ Find a state that has a higher per capita income than your state: _____

❹ Find a state that has a lower per capita income than your state: _____

GED Practice

Question 1 refers to the following map.

CENTRAL AMERICA

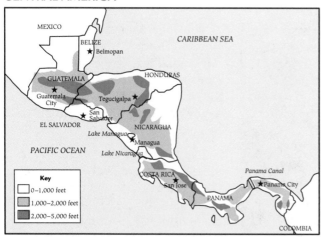

① Belmopan is the capital of Belize. The elevation of Belmopan is most similar to

  ① Washington, D.C., the United States capital, which is near sea level

  ② Denver, known as the Mile High City because it is one mile above sea level

  ③ Death Valley, with the lowest point in the U.S., over 200 feet below sea level

  ④ Mount McKinley, the highest point in the U.S., over 20,000 feet

  ⑤ Loveland Pass, on the Continental Divide, elevation 11,990 feet

Question 2 is based on the following map.

THE LAST ANCIENT FORESTS OF NORTH AMERICA

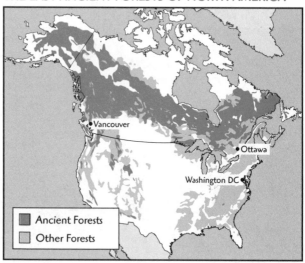

② Which of the following statements is supported by the information in this map?

  ① The United States and Canada have about the same amount of ancient forest.

  ② The conservation movement has been more effective in the U.S. than in Canada.

  ③ Canada has preserved much more of its ancient forest than the United States.

  ④ The eastern United States has the most ancient forest in North America.

  ⑤ Because of its cold climate, Alaska has less ancient forest than the rest of the U.S.

24

Applying Given Ideas

A map can contain important ideas that can be applied to people's actions or their understandings of the world.

WORLD VIEW OF PLATE TECTONICS

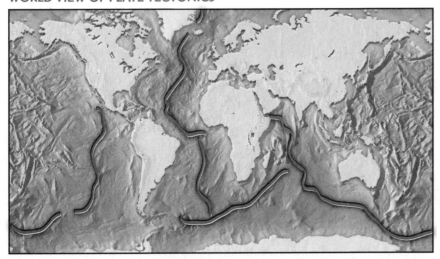

This map, known as the Heezen/Tharp World Ocean Floor Panorama, was one of the earliest maps to give a complete picture of the ocean floor. What important idea was strongly supported by this map?

The theory of Continental Drift seemed far more likely to be true given the evidence on this map. In particular, the mid-Atlantic ridge made it look very likely that Africa was joined to the Americas at one time.

The following map shows total water use across the United States in 1990.

TOTAL WATER WITHDRAWALS IN THE UNITED STATES IN 1990

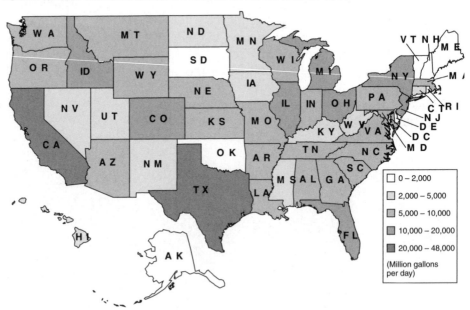

❶ If you are a farmer in Texas, what is this map telling you?

_____

❷ If you own a tree farm in Wyoming, what is this map telling you?

_____

GED Practice

Question 1 refers to the following map.

CALIFORNIA FAULT LINES

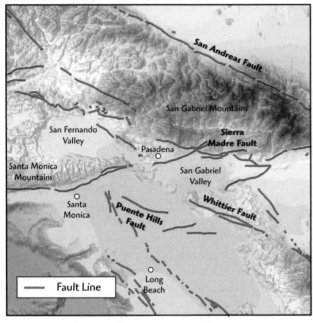

① The map above shows fault lines in the Los Angeles, California, area. Which idea is supported by this map?

  ① Buildings in Los Angeles are all earthquake resistant.
  ② Major gas pipelines can be safely built in the Los Angeles area.
  ③ Los Angeles public safety departments need to plan for a disaster.
  ④ Many areas in greater Los Angeles are safe from an earthquake.
  ⑤ New highways would help evacuate Los Angeles in an emergency.

Question 2 is based on the following map.

MAP OF UNITED STATES CORNBELT

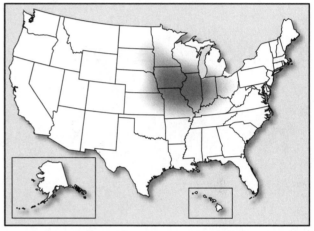

② All of the following would be applications of this map except

  ① maintaining a produce inspection system throughout the highlighted area
  ② restoring the prairie to its natural state throughout the highlighted area
  ③ promoting a program to buy development rights for farmland in the highlighted area
  ④ planning a factory in the highlighted area to produce ethanol from corn waste
  ⑤ developing a new corn storage facility within the highlighted area

Judging the Adequacy of Facts

Look at the following map of the Persian Empire and the Greek city-states in the fifth century B.C. During this period, the Persian Empire attacked the Greek city-states with massive armies and navies. Looking at the map, what would you expect would be the outcome of such an invasion?

MAP OF PERSIAN EMPIRE AND GREEK CITY-STATES

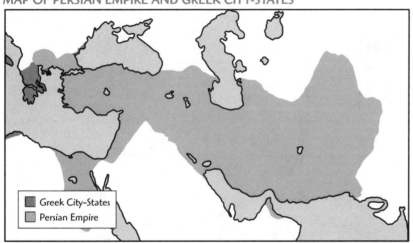

Greek City-States
Persian Empire

Based on the map, you might expect that the Greeks had no chance against the huge Persian Empire. Yet that is not what happened; the Greeks defeated the Persians. By itself, the map did not give you adequate information to make a decision.

When you look at a map, you need to evaluate what the map can and cannot tell you. The map on the left can tell you that the Persian Empire was far larger than the Greek city-states. But that alone is not enough to make a prediction of the outcome of a war between them.

Now look at this map of the level of uncollected fines in the United States.

TOTAL BALANCE OF FINES OWED TO U.S. ATTORNEYS (2004)

$20 million to $99 million
$100 million to $499 million
$500 million to $999 million
$1 billion to $9 billion

D.C.
Guam
Puerto Rico

❶ What can you state based on the information on this map?

_____

❷ What additional information might you need in order to determine why some states have such high uncollected fines and others have much lower amounts?

_____

_____

GED Practice

Question 1 refers to the following map.

NATIVE AMERICANS OF NORTH AMERICA

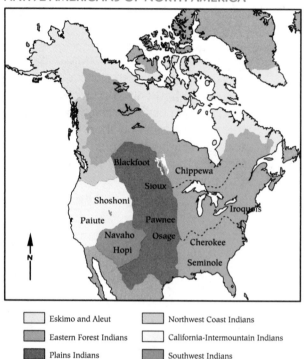

1. There is sufficient information in this map to determine that

   (1) the Eskimo and Aleut Indians inhabited all of North America
   (2) the Plains Indians were the strongest of all the groups
   (3) the California-Intermountain Indians thrived because of the climate and resources in their area
   (4) the Eastern Forest Indians were the largest group in North America
   (5) the Southwest Indians' territory was growing larger as they conquered other tribes

Question 2 is based on the following map.

MILWAUKEE AND VICINITY

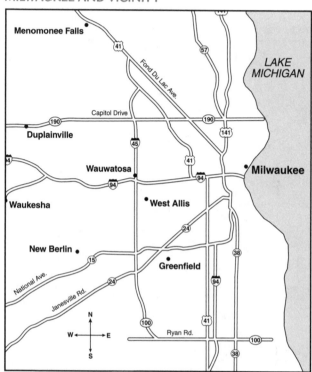

2. The information on this map is adequate to determine

   (1) the best areas to live in metropolitan Milwaukee
   (2) that I-94 is the best route to avoid traffic congestion in Milwaukee
   (3) the need for new multi-lane highways in the metropolitan Milwaukee region
   (4) how to get from Menomonee Falls to Waukesha
   (5) the best time of day to use Highway Route 24

Drawing Conclusions

A map can contain information that allows you to **draw conclusions** about the areas depicted in the map. Look at the following map of Nepal. What conclusions can you draw about the road system?

MAP OF NEPAL

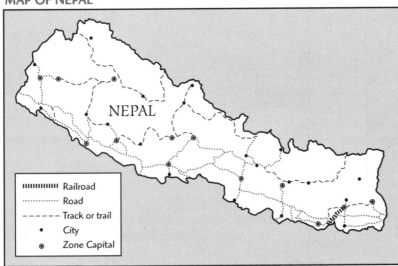

NEPAL

|||||||||| Railroad
.... Road
– – – – Track or trail
• City
◉ Zone Capital

If you look closely at the map, you can see that many towns only have tracks or trails going through them. You can conclude that the road system is not very good or complete. You might also notice that there is only one short railroad line near the southeast border. You can conclude that there is little rail transportation in Nepal.

CENTRAL/EASTERN ARCTIC AREA

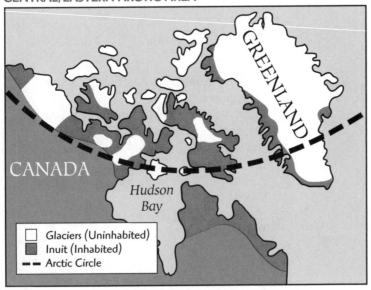

GREENLAND

CANADA

Hudson Bay

☐ Glaciers (Uninhabited)
▨ Inuit (Inhabited)
– – Arctic Circle

Now look at the map of northern Canada and Greenland on the left.

❶ What conclusions can you draw about the climate in this area?

_____

_____

_____

❷ What conclusions can you draw about this area's main inhabitants, the Inuit?

_____

_____

_____

GED Practice

Question 1 refers to the following map of Europe during World War II.

CASUALTIES IN WWII BY COUNTRY

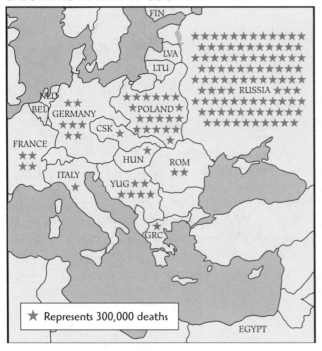

★ Represents 300,000 deaths

1. What is a conclusion that you can draw from this map?

   (1) World War II was the bloodiest war in human history.
   (2) During World War II, most of the people were killed in Europe.
   (3) The United States made the greatest sacrifices during World War II.
   (4) The Jews of Europe were almost wiped out during World War II.
   (5) During World War II, more people died in Russia than anywhere else in Europe.

Question 2 is based on the two maps of Milwaukee. On the left is a map of light intensity during the night. On the right is a map of population density for the area with the most light intensity.

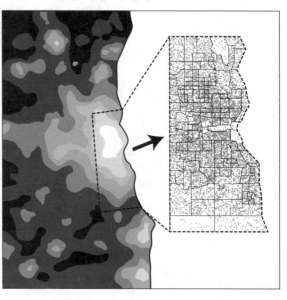

2. Using the two maps, you can conclude

   (1) Milwaukee is one of the largest cities in the United States
   (2) higher density areas tend to have the most light pollution
   (3) Milwaukee needs to severely restrict the use of outdoor lighting
   (4) the population of the Milwaukee area is slowly increasing
   (5) Milwaukee needs to do a better job of lighting its coastal areas

Distinguishing Fact from Opinion

A map can convey both facts and opinions. A **fact** is something that can be proved or disproved. An **opinion** is a statement of a feeling that cannot be completely proved or disproved.

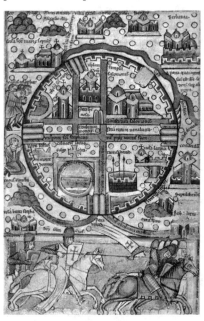

To the left is a crusader map of Jerusalem created in the twelfth century. Why do you think the mapmaker drew Jerusalem as a perfect circle?

We can only guess why Jerusalem was drawn as a perfect circle. It might be because Jerusalem was considered a holy city, so the mapmaker wanted it to look perfect. We can only have an opinion about the mapmaker's motives since no written record survives. Today, some people think this map is a beautiful memory of an ancient romantic time. Others might consider the map and the artwork hard to understand and out-of-date. Both of these points of view are opinions.

INSURGENCIES IN IRAQ

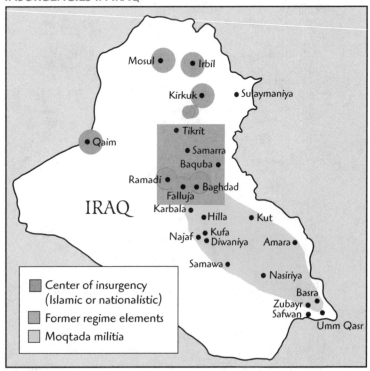

Now look at the map of Iraq on the left.

❶ After each of the following statements, write whether it is a fact that can be drawn from the map or an opinion.

① Baghdad is a center of insurgency. _____

② The United States forces are defeating the insurgency. _____

③ The Moqtada militia is most powerful in southeast Iraq. _____

④ The insurgency is spreading and has popular support. _____

⑤ Large areas of Iraq are relatively free of insurgents. _____

GED Practice

Question 1 refers to the following map.

WHALES AND MILITARY SONAR

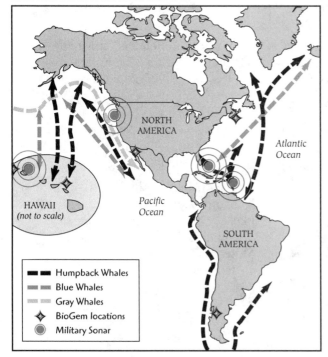

1. Based on the information in the map, which of the following is an opinion?

   (1) Military sonar should be severely restricted in order to protect whales.
   (2) Whales migrate through areas where military sonar is used.
   (3) Blue whales can be found in the Atlantic Ocean and in the Pacific Ocean.
   (4) Military sonar is used in the Atlantic Ocean and in the Pacific Ocean.
   (5) Humpback whales migrate up the east and west coasts of South America.

Question 2 is based on the following map.

COLD WAR ALLIANCES

☐ NATO
☐ Warsaw Pact, 1955–1991

2. Based on the map, all of the following are facts except

   (1) NATO and the Warsaw Pact each controlled a large amount of territory
   (2) North African countries were not members of NATO or the Warsaw Pact
   (3) NATO was a stronger alliance than the Warsaw Pact
   (4) the United States and Canada were members of NATO
   (5) the Soviet Union was the largest nation in the Warsaw Pact

Summarizing the Main Idea

Political cartoons and photographs can convey powerful images and messages. In order to understand a political cartoon or photograph, you need to be able to describe in words what it is about. You need to be able to **summarize** the most important ideas conveyed by the image.

Look at the political cartoon on the left titled, "For the Championship of the United States." There are two figures facing each other. The larger one is labeled "Uncontrolled Campaign Spending." The smaller one is labeled "92nd Congress." Who do you think has the advantage in this fight?

The cartoon makes it very clear that "Uncontrolled Campaign Spending" is likely to defeat "Congress" for the championship, or control of the United States. This is the **main idea** of the cartoon.

Look at the following photograph of young coal miners in 1911.

➊ What do you think is the main idea of this photograph?

_____

_____

GED Practice

Question 1 refers to the following political cartoon from 1869.

[65]   August 7, 1869

Pacific Chivalry.
Encouragement to Chinese immigration.

1 The main idea of this political cartoon is

   (1) Chinese immigration needs to be encouraged

   (2) the Chinese need to adopt Western-style dress

   (3) the Chinese should not be welcome in California

   (4) California is abusing its Chinese immigrants

   (5) the Chinese and the Californians need to work out their differences

Question 2 is based on the following photograph taken of Jewish Holocaust survivors in 1945.

2 Which of the following best expresses the main idea of this photograph?

   (1) Human beings are capable of almost unbelievable cruelty.

   (2) The Jewish Holocaust survivors had been starved and mistreated.

   (3) The Holocaust was one of the greatest crimes in human history.

   (4) This terrible mistreatment of human beings must never happen again.

   (5) The Nazis need to be hunted down and punished for their crimes.

Identifying Implications

Political cartoons use images to make **implications.** What can you imply about the war in Iraq from the following cartoon?

A mirage is something that you see in the desert that isn't really there. Therefore, you can imply from this cartoon that there is no exit strategy for the war in Iraq.

In the following cartoon, EPA stands for the Environmental Protection Agency and DNR stands for the Department of Natural Resources.

❶ Unless you live in Wisconsin or Illinois, you might not know much about the Fox River. What does the cartoon imply about the Fox River?

_____

❷ What does the cartoon imply about the plan to clean up the Fox River?

_____

GED Practice

Question 1 refers to the following political cartoon.

1 An implication of this cartoon is

   ① gasoline pumps can be very dangerous

   ② high gas prices are strangling the United States

   ③ there might be a shortage of gasoline in the U.S.

   ④ we need to worry about our future supplies of gas

   ⑤ gas taxes need to be lowered so that Americans can drive more

Question 2 is based on the following photograph taken of the Driving of the Golden Spike in 1869. The ceremony marked the completion of the Transcontinental Railroad.

2 It can be inferred from this photograph that

   ① the participants were well aware of the importance of the event

   ② the two trains came dangerously close to crashing into each other

   ③ it was a common practice to celebrate the completion of a railroad line

   ④ the workers had been treated well during the construction project

   ⑤ the people in the scene were unaware that they were being photographed

Applying Remembered Ideas

Political cartoons often depend upon **remembered ideas,** or stories. What story is this cartoon of Nelson Mandela's retirement referring to?

This cartoon refers to the story of Moses leading the Israelites to the Promised Land. In the cartoon, Nelson Mandela has led the people of South Africa to the Promised Land of Freedom and Democracy. The cartoonist hopes that while Mandela gets a well-deserved rest, South African society will be transformed from its sad past.

The following cartoon depends on the reader knowing a famous children's classic.

1 What is the story that is being referred to in this cartoon?

_____

2 What does the cartoonist want you to believe about the cigarette company executives?

_____

GED Practice

Question 1 refers to the following political cartoon.

1 The title of the above cartoon is "Thanksgiving Day, 1884." The man outside the window is carrying a turkey labeled "Presidency." The dinner plate has a crow. All of the following are probably true except

  ① the man carrying the turkey had unexpectedly won the presidency

  ② the men around the table were supporters of the new president

  ③ the men around the table were disappointed by the election results

  ④ the men had expected to celebrate their victory

  ⑤ the men are not eager to eat what is on the dinner plate

Question 2 is based on the following political cartoon.

2 The image of the four horsemen is being used to suggest that

  ① in a competitive world, e-mail can be a powerful advantage

  ② the leading software companies are racing to control e-mail

  ③ e-mail is being threatened with total destruction

  ④ the free market has led to new uses of e-mail

  ⑤ e-mail is trying to stay ahead of its problems

Applying Given Ideas

Political cartoons and photographs can show us compelling images that we can apply to our own perceptions and actions.

The following image is a photograph of an old woman in front of a department store window during the Great Depression. The title of the photograph is "One Third of the Nation." If you were wealthy and saw this photograph when it was first taken, how might you have applied its message?

This image might make you more aware of the poor and more willing to help them. You also might be stricken by the contrast between the old woman and the mannequin and decide to be less selfish and more thoughtful of others.

The following cartoon is from 1904 when Teddy Roosevelt was running for reelection as president.

UNCLE SAM: "He's good enough for me."

1 In the cartoon, what does Uncle Sam think of Teddy Roosevelt?

_____

2 If you were a voter in 1904 and agreed with this cartoon, what would you do?

_____

GED Practice

Question 1 refers to the following political cartoon.

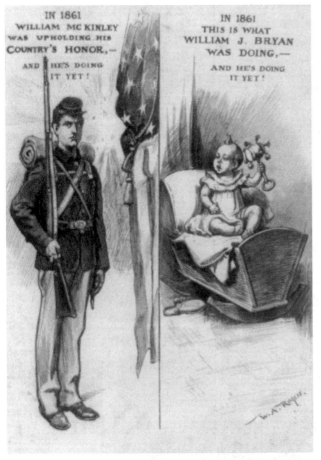

IN 1861 WILLIAM MCKINLEY WAS UPHOLDING HIS COUNTRY'S HONOR,— AND HE'S DOING IT YET!

IN 1861 THIS IS WHAT WILLIAM J. BRYAN WAS DOING,— AND HE'S DOING IT YET!

THE DEADLY PARALLEL.

1 This cartoon is from 1861. If you were reading this cartoon at the time, what could it motivate you to do?

  (1) start a family
  (2) join the army
  (3) give up hope for the future
  (4) support world peace
  (5) travel the world

Question 2 is based on the following political cartoon.

2 If a reader were to apply the message of the above cartoon, he or she would most likely

  (1) try to always appear natural
  (2) get super-sized meal portions
  (3) treat the dead with respect
  (4) be buried with personal possessions
  (5) eat healthier and exercise more

Distinguishing Fact from Opinion

When reading a political cartoon, it is important to be able to distinguish fact from opinion. Usually, the purpose of a political cartoon is to express a strong **opinion**, and a good cartoonist will use powerful images to convey that opinion.

Look at the following political cartoon. What is the **fact** that the cartoon is commenting upon? What is the opinion of the cartoonist?

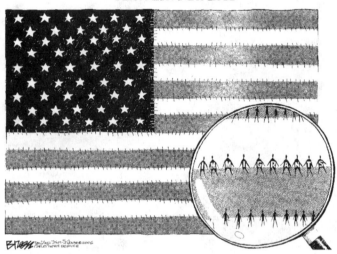

OUR NATIONAL FABRIC

The cartoonist is commenting on the fact that in March 2006, when he drew this cartoon, immigration reform was a major issue. His opinion about immigrants is that they are a part of our national fabric. Because they are the "stitches" that are keeping the flag together, it is clear that he sees immigrants as an essential part of the United States.

The following cartoon is from March 2006, when the top two executives from the bankrupt company Enron were on trial. They were accused of being involved in schemes to hide the true financial health of the company.

ENRON'S NEW EXECUTIVE SUITE

1 What does the cartoonist do in order to let you know his opinion about Enron?

_____

2 What is the cartoonist's opinion?

_____

GED Practice

Question 1 refers to the following political cartoon.

1 Which of the following is a fact?

(1) Minors facing execution should be treated kindly.

(2) The execution of minors is inhumane and wrong.

(3) The Supreme Court ruled that the execution of minors is unconstitutional.

(4) Prisons do a good job of preparing minors for execution.

(5) The Constitution should be amended to allow the execution of minors.

Question 2 is based on the following political cartoon.

2 This cartoon is from 1915 before women had the right to vote. The man comes home from work to find his wife gone and his children alone. A "Votes for Women" sign is on the wall. Under it is a note that reads, "Back some time this evening." What is the opinion about women's suffrage that the cartoon is trying to convey?

(1) When women vote, men will be expected to help out more around the house.

(2) When women have the right to vote, they will neglect their children and home.

(3) The right to vote will lead to women making valuable contributions to society.

(4) The needs of children and families will be addressed when women can vote.

(5) When women vote, men will have to work harder to support their families.

Recognizing Persuasive Information

A political cartoonist or photojournalist will use powerful images in order to **persuade**.

In the 1940s, as men were being shipped away to serve in World War II, many factories were left empty. The government designed this poster of "Rosie the Riveter" to recruit housewives to leave their homes and take over the heavy manufacturing jobs.

Spurred by this poster, millions of American women took higher-paying jobs in the war-production industry, such as assembling bombs, building tanks, and welding. Using the icon of a strong woman, the government persuaded women to join the war industry as their patriotic duty.

The following photograph is of the first airplane flight by the Wright brothers, Orville and Wilbur.

❶ Why do you think it was so important for the Wright Brothers to have a photograph taken of their airplane in flight?

_____

GED Practice

Question 1 refers to the following photograph.

1 Neil Armstrong took this picture of Buzz Aldrin when they were the first men to step foot on the moon on July 20, 1969. What has been the most important impact of this picture for NASA?

  (1) It generated tremendous support for the space program.

  (2) It encouraged NASA to develop see-through face visors.

  (3) It made people realize that there was little of value on the moon.

  (4) It became the most popular poster sold by the space agency.

  (5) It convinced the public to support manned exploration of Mars.

Question 2 is based on the following photograph.

2 On December 7, 1941, the Japanese attacked Pearl Harbor, crippling the American Pacific fleet. This image is of the USS *Arizona* after it was hit. What was the most important impact of these images on Americans?

  (1) It made people fear that the Japanese would soon invade the West Coast.

  (2) Americans were frustrated that our intelligence had not predicted the attack.

  (3) Support for building new ships declined because they would not last long.

  (4) Americans supported going to war with Japan and its allies, Germany and Italy.

  (5) Americans became convinced that war was not a reasonable solution to disputes.

Understanding the Photographer's or Cartoonist's Purpose

In the early 1870s, no one knew if a horse ever had all four hooves in the air while it was galloping. Leland Stanford asked photographer Eadweard Muybridge if he could figure out a way to answer this question. Muybridge's solution was to set up a series of cameras along a track. As the horse and rider passed each camera, they broke a trip wire that caused the picture to be taken.

The series of pictures is shown on the left. The photographer's **purpose** was to prove whether or not all of a horse's hooves are off the ground at the same time while it is galloping. Did the pictures answer the question?

If you look at the second and third pictures in the first row, you can clearly see that all four hooves are off the ground at the same time.

The Horse in Motion
—Eadweard Muybridge

The following cartoon was drawn by Thomas Nast in 1868. The title of the cartoon is "The Modern Samson." The woman in the cartoon is holding Samson's cut hair, which is labeled "suffrage," or the right to vote.

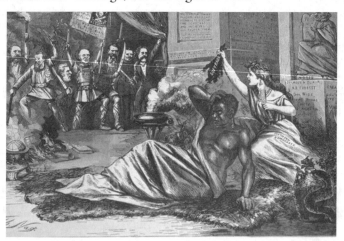

1 What happened to Samson when his hair was cut?

_____

2 In this cartoon, who is the modern Samson?

_____

3 What do you think was Nast's purpose when he drew this cartoon?

_____

GED Practice

Question 1 refers to the following photograph.

1 Toward the end of World War II, American troops attacked the Japanese island of Iwo Jima. This photograph was taken as a group of soldiers raised the American flag on the island. What was most likely the photographer's purpose in taking this photograph?

  (1) He wanted to create a model for a World War II memorial.

  (2) He wanted to reassure the public that soldiers respected the flag.

  (3) He wanted to show the hard-won victory of American soldiers.

  (4) He wanted to discourage the Japanese and convince them to surrender.

  (5) He wanted to show how difficult it was to raise the American flag.

Question 2 is based on the following political cartoon.

2 The cartoonist's purpose in drawing this cartoon is most likely to

  (1) show the power of the Populist Party over the Democratic Party

  (2) point out that William Jennings Bryan is a snake

  (3) rally support for the Democratic Party

  (4) point out that political parties never get along

  (5) criticize the Democratic Party

Recognizing Unstated Assumptions

This photograph of a young Jewish boy's arrest by the Nazis is a powerful and haunting image.

Part of its power lies in the **unstated assumption** that when dangerous criminals are caught, they need to hold up their hands so that they cannot attack their captor. Yet it is obvious that this young boy is no danger or threat to anyone.

The following cartoon was drawn by Herb Block in 1954. The man climbing out of the sewer is Richard Nixon, who at the time was vice president of the United States.

❶ What do you think is Herbert Block's opinion of Richard Nixon?

_____

❷ What are some assumptions that Block uses to help make his opinion clear?

_____

_____

GED Practice

Question 1 refers to the following political cartoon.

"Hi. My name is Barry, and I check my E-mail two to three hundred times a day."

1 Which of the following is an unstated assumption that is the source of the humor in this cartoon?

  ① People like to talk about their computer problems to groups of friends.

  ② E-mail can become an uncontrollable addiction for some people.

  ③ The 12-step program of Alcoholics Anonymous can be used for other addictions.

  ④ Alcoholism has been replaced by use of e-mail as a serious addiction problem.

  ⑤ Many people are having a hard time keeping their e-mail use under control.

Question 2 is based on the following political cartoon.

2 Which of the following is an unstated assumption of the cartoonist?

  ① We do not have enough money to properly support our troops.

  ② There is no relationship between tax rates and military spending.

  ③ Americans are likely to donate their tax savings to the military.

  ④ It is easier to keep a vehicle running properly in the U.S. than in Iraq.

  ⑤ Spending your tax cut is the best way to show support for our troops.

Identifying Cause and Effect Relationships

What is the **cause and effect relationship** in the cartoon below?

Most produce in the United States is picked by immigrant farm workers. U.S. workers would be paid much more than immigrant workers, which would cause the cost of produce to increase dramatically. The cost of $20 for three oranges is the effect of having U.S. workers handpicking them.

Cartoonists often create a humorous image when they exaggerate a cause and effect relationship.

❶ What is the cause and effect relationship being exaggerated in this cartoon?

_____

GED Practice

Question 1 refers to the following cartoon.

"I'm sorry, but you're going to have to hand over that cape. Your test came back positive for anabolic steroids."

1 What is the cause and effect relationship that this cartoon is addressing?

(1) Superheroes must be held to higher standards, because their behavior affects kids.

(2) Using special drugs helps athletes perform better by increasing their muscle mass.

(3) If someone breaks the law, he or she needs to be punished no matter who he or she is.

(4) Over-regulation is limiting the tools available to law enforcement.

(5) Suspicion of substance abuse justifies compromising privacy rights.

Question 2 is based on the following political cartoon.

BENNETT THE CHRISTIAN SCIENCE MONITOR

2 According to the above cartoon, what will be the effect of an increasing debt?

(1) It will wreck the economic recovery.

(2) The economy will continue to grow.

(3) It will give Americans something to celebrate.

(4) It will be controlled by economic planning.

(5) It will be ignored by the American public.

Recognizing the Cartoonist's or Photographer's Point of View

Everybody has a **point of view.** Look at the cartoon below. How do you think the small fish arrived at its point of view? How about the large fish and the medium fish?

MANKOFF

The smallest fish is always the victim, so its point of view is that there is no justice in the world. The largest fish is never threatened. It just preys on smaller and weaker fish, so from its point of view, the world is just. The fish is the middle sometimes preys on smaller fish and is sometimes preyed upon by larger ones, so it believes that there is some justice in the world.

Look at the following political cartoon that was drawn when the United States first adopted the graduated income tax after World War I.

Men of Large Incomes are "Seeing Things"

1 What is the point of view of the men in the boat?

_____

2 What do you think is the point of view of the cartoonist?

_____

3 What evidence did you use to come to your conclusions?

_____

GED Practice

Question 1 refers to the following photograph.

1 This photograph shows Russian citizens with a fallen statue of Felix Edmundovich Dzerzhinsky, the founder of the KGB, the Russian secret police, in 1991. Which of the following best describes the point of view of the photographer?

  ① outrage at the disrespect being shown to the hero of the KGB

  ② presenting a balanced and unbiased view of the events in Russia

  ③ presenting a nostalgic view of a passionate past destroyed by small-minded people

  ④ appreciation of the symbolic importance of ordinary Russians with the statue

  ⑤ excitement about the opportunity to take an award-winning photograph

Question 2 is based on the following political cartoon.

2 What is most likely the point of view of the cartoonist who drew the above cartoon?

  ① The United States needs to be more welcoming at the border.

  ② The current border policy of the United States is working well.

  ③ The United States is ineffective at keeping out illegal immigrants.

  ④ The United States needs to provide illegal immigrants with a path to citizenship.

  ⑤ The border policy of the United States is scaring off good workers.

Recognizing Historical Context

Many young people without knowledge of recent history would have a hard time understanding the following political cartoon.

"We never go anywhere but West Berlin."

West Berlin was entirely surrounded by the Berlin Wall, which separated it from East Germany. Prior to the tearing down of the wall in 1989, drivers in West Berlin could not travel beyond the wall. Only in its **historical context** does this cartoon make sense.

Many political cartoons are set in a particular place and time. Look at the following cartoon and see if you can figure out its historical context.

1 What are the two activities the woman is doing?

_____

2 What time in American history would these actions appear to be taking place?

_____

3 What evidence is there of the time and place of the cartoon?

_____

Question 1 refers to the following political cartoon.

"Now, if you don't come down, I'll cut the tree from under you."

1 This political cartoon was created at what time in United States history?

  ① at the beginning of the American Revolution against the British

  ② during the Constitutional Convention when the Constitution was written

  ③ towards the end of the Mexican War, when the U.S. took Mexican territory

  ④ while the North was fighting the South in the Civil War to preserve the Union

  ⑤ when the United States entered World War II to fight against fascism

Question 2 is based on the following political cartoon.

2 When this cartoon was drawn in 2001, what current situation was it commenting about?

  ① an extreme Islamic fundamentalist government in Afghanistan

  ② a return to traditional family and gender values around the world

  ③ America's obsessions with sexuality and material possessions

  ④ the proliferation of specialized magazines appealing to narrow groups

  ⑤ the wild and unpredictable swings in current styles in women's fashions

Identifying Comparisons and Contrasts

Political cartoons and photographs often use **comparisons** and **contrasts** to have an impact or make a point. Look at the cartoon below. What is the contrast in the cartoon?

Equality should mean "open to all," yet the door says, "authorized personnel only," which means "only open to a select few."

Often, political cartoons or photographs can contain both comparisons and contrasts. Look at the following political cartoon of President George W. Bush.

❶ Who is President Bush being compared to?

_____

❷ What is the contrast in the cartoon?

_____

❸ What does the cartoonist want you to think about the National Security Agency's wiretaps authorized by President Bush?

_____

GED Practice

Question 1 refers to the following political cartoon.

*"There's money enough to support both of you...
Now, doesn't that make you feel better?"*

Question 2 is based on the following photograph.

1 What is the contrast this cartoon is trying to illustrate?

(1) the contrast between the glamorous clothes of the wealthy and the old clothes of the poor

(2) the contrast of a businesslike administration trying to control a wasteful and expensive war

(3) the contrast of the current difference between funding of the war and urban needs and future promises

(4) the contrast between the overweight, gaudy woman and the thin, poor woman

(5) the contrast between huge amounts of money to support the war versus small amounts for urban needs

2 The photograph above illustrates all of the following contrasts except

(1) old buildings versus new buildings

(2) dull architecture versus exciting architecture

(3) large buildings versus small buildings

(4) stone construction versus glass and concrete construction

(5) high-rise towers versus a low-rise building

Recognizing Values

Visual images can convey **values**. The values could be those of the artist or of the subject of the work. What are the values expressed in the following cartoon?

Friendship and responsibility are the values expressed in the cartoon. As the dog looks at its empty bowl, it thinks that its owner is not acting like a pal when he forgets to feed it.

Often in political cartoons, the values of the characters in the cartoon do not match the values of the artist.

"It really shook me, I can tell you. I dreamed the meek inherited the earth!"

❶ What do you think the values are of the generals in the cartoon?

_____

❷ What do you think the values are of the cartoonist?

_____

❸ What was your reasoning in answering the first two questions?

_____

GED Practice

Question 1 refers to the following political cartoon.

"Then ask yourselves, 'Do we really <u>need</u> all this luxury?' And your answer, of course, is Yes!"

1 The real estate agent assumes that the couple shares which of his values?

(1) charity
(2) empathy
(3) patriotism
(4) responsibility
(5) materialism

Question 2 is based on the following photograph.

2 What value is most clearly expressed in this photograph?

(1) love
(2) charity
(3) grief
(4) respect
(5) wealth

Determining the Implications and Effects of Values

Values have an impact. Cartoonists or photographers often create images that illustrate the **implications** and **effects** of values. According to the following cartoon, what is one of the effects of living in a democracy?

"We can't come to an agreement about how to fix your car, Mr. Simons. Sometimes that's the way things happen in a democracy."

According to the cartoon, it can be hard to get things done in a democracy because everyone has a voice in decision making.

The following cartoon looks at the balance of freedom and security.

"Look, you've got to accept some curtailment of your freedom in exchange for increased security."

1 According to the cartoon, what is an effect of limiting freedom in exchange for increased security?

_____

2 Do you think that the cartoonist thinks this is a reasonable trade-off?

_____

3 What was your reasoning in answering the first two questions?

_____

GED Practice

Questions 1 and 2 refer to the following political cartoon.

1. What would be the implications for American policy if we followed the values of the man in the SUV?

   ① We would pay more attention to conservation.
   ② We would tax vehicles that are built outside the U.S.
   ③ We would rely on American ingenuity to help us.
   ④ We would do whatever it takes to get more oil.
   ⑤ We would support increasing subsidies for oil companies.

2. What would be the implications for American policy if we followed the values of the man in the vehicle labeled "energy alternatives"?

   ① We would pay more attention to conservation.
   ② We would tax vehicles that are built outside the U.S.
   ③ We would ban the use of large gas-guzzling vehicles.
   ④ We would do whatever it takes to get more oil.
   ⑤ We would support increasing subsidies for oil companies.

Question 3 is based on the following political cartoon.

3. In 2005, Hurricane Katrina devastated the Louisiana and Mississippi coasts. What values and implications related to that calamity does the cartoon illustrate?

   ① Reliance on government help leads to disaster.
   ② Resourcefulness can solve the most difficult problems.
   ③ Teamwork helps people get out of the toughest jams.
   ④ Selfishness at home exposes U.S. troops in Iraq to dangers.
   ⑤ Militarism leaves the U.S. unable to protect its own people.

Recognizing a Trend in Data

Tables, charts, and graphs can present a great deal of information in a small amount of space. Graphs can be very effective at illustrating a **trend in data**. Look at the following graph of world population. What was the trend in human population growth from the Old Stone Age to the beginning of the Modern Age? What has been the trend in human population growth during the Modern Age?

WORLD POPULATION GROWTH THROUGH HISTORY

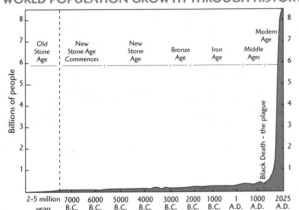

The line on the graph is almost flat from the Old Stone Age to the Modern Age, except for a dip during the Black Death. This line graph shows a very gradual increase in human population from the Old Stone Age to the beginning of the Modern Age. In the Modern Age, the line shifts dramatically upward, showing a rapid population increase. According to this line graph, the current trend in human population growth is a rapid increase.

Data can be presented as a table as well as in graph form. Look at the following graph and table. They are both presenting the same data.

TOTAL FERTILITY RATE(s) (avg. births per childbearing woman) in Bangladesh	
Year(s)	Fertility Rate
1950–1955	6.70
1955–1960	6.90
1960–1965	7.10
1965–1970	6.80
1970–1975	6.40
1975–1980	5.70
1980–1985	5.30
1985–1990	4.80
1990–1995	4.30
1995–2000	3.80

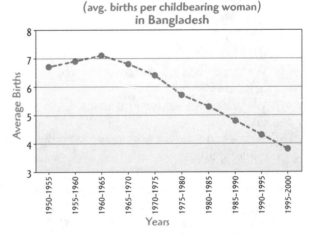

TOTAL FERTILITY RATE(s)
(avg. births per childbearing woman)
in Bangladesh

❶ In which form, table or graph, is it easier to find the exact rate for each time period?

_____

❷ In which form, table or graph, is it easier to see a trend?

_____

❸ Describe the trend since 1950 of fertility rates in Bangladesh.

_____

GED Practice

Question 1 refers to the following graph.

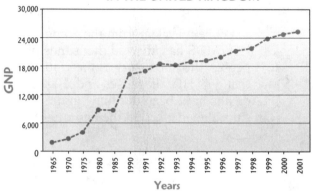

GNP PER CAPITA IN NOMINAL U.S. DOLLARS IN THE UNITED KINGDOM

① What would be the best description of the trend in the per capita gross national product in the United Kingdom from 1990 to 2000?

  ① The trend was a steady increase almost every year.
  ② There was no consistent trend during the entire period.
  ③ There was a steady increase except for two periods of rapid increases.
  ④ There was one small drop in one year during the 1990s.
  ⑤ Adjusted for inflation, GNP was steady for the decade.

Questions 2 and 3 are based on the following table.

CHANGE IN FOREST COVER 1990–2005			
Continent	Total Forest 1990	Total Forest 2005	Change 1990–2005
	Million Hectares		Percent
Africa	699	635	-4.3
Asia	574	572	-0.2
Oceania	213	206	-0.4
Europe	989	1,001	+0.8
North and Central America	711	706	-0.3
South America	891	832	-4.0
TOTAL WORLD	**4,077**	**3,952**	**-8.4**

Note: Percentages are based on non-rounded area measurements.
Source: U.N. Food and Agriculture Organization, Global Forest Resources Assessment 2005

② Which region was not following the worldwide trend in change in forest cover?

  ① Africa
  ② Asia
  ③ Europe
  ④ North and Central America
  ⑤ South America

③ Which of the following is the trend shown in the table?

  ① Africa shows an increase in forest cover while Asia shows a decrease.
  ② Almost all countries show a decrease in forest cover.
  ③ Almost all countries show an increase in forest cover.
  ④ North and Central America show a decrease in forest cover while South America shows an increase.
  ⑤ The table does not show a trend.

Summarizing the Main Idea

A table or graph can be more than a collection of numbers or data points. It can also tell a story. Just as a reading passage or a political cartoon has a **main idea**, so can a table or graph. Look at the following bar graph and see if you can figure out the most important story that it has to tell. That will be the main idea of the graph.

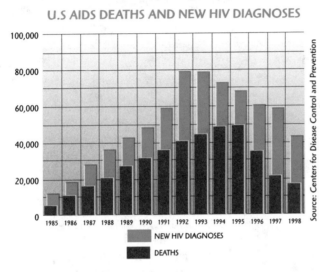

While it is clear from the graph that HIV/AIDS has affected thousands of people, the main story of the graph is that new HIV diagnoses and AIDS deaths have been declining in the U.S. since they peaked in the early 1990s.

The graph below shows the yearly income of a minimum wage job (adjusted for inflation) and the poverty line. The yearly income was calculated by multiplying the minimum wage by a work year of fifty 40-hour weeks.

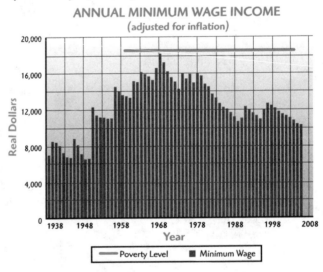

❶ What is the main idea of the graph?

_____

❷ What reasoning did you use to determine the main idea?

_____

GED Practice

Question 1 refers to the following graph.

CELLULAR PHONE SUBSCRIPTIONS
per 1,000 people in Australia and Nigeria

	Australia 639.5 (2002)	Nigeria 13.1 (2002)

(bar graph with y-axis values: 700, 560, 420, 280, 140, 0)

1 The main idea of the chart is

① the majority of people in Australia have subscriptions for cellular phones

② very few people in Nigeria have subscriptions for cellular phones

③ every year, more people are buying subscriptions for cellular phones

④ cellular phones are becoming more popular than regular land line phones

⑤ a much greater percentage of Australians use cellular phones than Nigerians

Question 2 is based on the following table.

WORLD WAR II MILITARY DEATHS
(Allies)

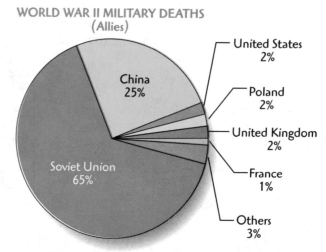

2 What is the main idea of this chart?

① China and the Soviet Union were allies of the U.S. in World War II.

② The United States was the leader of the allies in World War II.

③ All of the allies had many soldiers killed during World War II.

④ The Soviet Union lost more soldiers than the rest of the allies combined.

⑤ More soldiers were killed in World War II than in any other conflict in history.

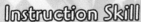

Identifying Implications

You can draw **implications** from a table or graph just as you can from a reading passage, map, political cartoon, or photograph. Look at the following table of apparel manufacturing employment in five southern states. What is an implication you can draw from this table?

APPAREL MANUFACTURING EMPLOYMENT (in thousands)			
	1990	2000	2005
Alabama	60.4	28.9	15.2
Mississippi	34.3	31.1	4.9
North Carolina	98.4	48.1	25.9
South Carolina	37.6	10.5	3.6
Tennessee	64.0	20.4	8.5

Source: U.S. Bureau of Labor Statistics

You could infer that apparel manufacturing employment was declining throughout the South because every state had major declines over a fifteen-year period. Another implication that you can draw is that the decline will likely continue and apparel manufacturing employment in these states will continue to drop.

The following table gives population projections in Texas under two scenarios. In the first, there is zero net migration. In other words, the same number of people moves into the state as the number that moves out. In the second scenario, net migration stays about the same as it was from 1990–2000.

TEXAS POPULATION PROJECTIONS BY RACE/ETHNICITY FROM 2000 TO 2040					
Year	Anglo	Black	Hispanic	Other	Total
Assuming Zero Net Migration					
2000	11,074,716	2,421,653	6,669,666	685,785	20,851,820
2010	11,292,858	2,604,162	7,986,640	776,088	22,659,748
2020	11,320,857	2,727,365	9,229,971	828,786	24,097,979
2030	11,086,475	2,756,470	10,406,060	856,437	25,105,442
2040	10,599,190	2,697,888	11,408,456	856,047	25,561,581
Assuming Net Migration Equal to 1990–2000					
2000	11,074,716	2,421,653	6,669,666	685,785	20,851,820
2010	11,700,471	2,863,397	10,164,378	1,168,772	25,897,018
2020	12,165,004	3,309,068	15,056,028	1,897182	32,427,282
2030	12,350,427	3,694,283	21,533,219	2,960,361	40,538,290
2040	12,225,486	3,995,349	29,926,210	4,435,916	50,582,961

❶ What is the implication of this table regarding the racial and ethnic backgrounds of Texans by the middle of the twenty-first century?

GED Practice

Question 1 refers to the following graphs and passage.

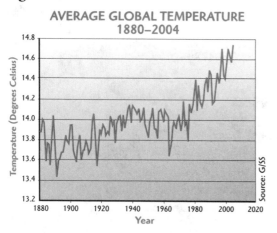

AVERAGE GLOBAL TEMPERATURE
1880–2004

Source: GISS

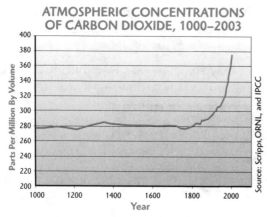

ATMOSPHERIC CONCENTRATIONS
OF CARBON DIOXIDE, 1000–2003

Source: Scripps, ORNL, and IPCC

Most scientists now believe that increasing concentrations of carbon dioxide in the atmosphere are causing increasing global temperatures. Burning fossil fuels and cutting down forests are the two main ways that carbon dioxide is released to the atmosphere.

1 What is an implication of the carbon dioxide graph and the short passage?

(1) People will never be willing to give up their comforts to stop global warming.

(2) Global warming will continue at a faster rate in the twenty-first century.

(3) The atmospheric concentration of carbon dioxide will level off soon.

(4) People will soon realize they must stop using fossil fuels and cutting down forests.

(5) Drastic changes in the atmosphere will make it harder for many people to breathe.

Question 2 is based on the following table.

THE TEN FASTEST-GROWING METROPOLITAN AREAS 1990–2000				
Metropolitan Area	Population		Change, 1990–2000	
	April 1, 1990	April 1, 2000	Number	Percent
Las Vegas, Nev., Ariz.	852,737	1,563,282	710,545	83.3%
Naples, Fla.	152,099	251,377	99,278	65.3
Yuma, Ariz.	106,895	160,026	53,131	49.7
McAllen-Edinburg-Mission, Tex.	383,545	569,463	185,918	48.5
Austin-San Marcos, Tex.	846,227	1,249,763	403,536	47.7
Fayetteville-Springdale-Rogers, Ark.	210,908	311,121	100,213	47.5
Boise, Idaho	295,851	432,345	136,494	46.1
Phoenix-Mesa, Ariz.	2,238,480	3,251,876	1,013,396	45.3
Laredo, Tex.	133,239	193,117	59,878	44.9
Provo-Orem, Utah	263,590	368,536	104,946	39.8

Source: U.S. Census Bureau, Census 2000: 1990 Census. Web: www.census.gov

2 An implication of this table is that

(1) states in the South and West are becoming overcrowded

(2) the Northeast and Midwest are losing people to the South and West

(3) the South and West will continue to be the fastest growing areas of the U.S

(4) population growth in the United States is impossible to control

(5) metropolitan areas in the South and West can handle very rapid growth

Applying Information Given

The information in a table or graph is often meant to be used or **applied** to real life situations.

How would you apply the information given in the following graph?

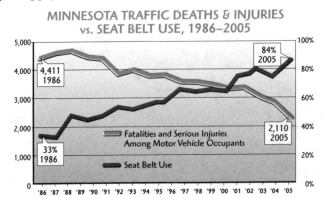

MINNESOTA TRAFFIC DEATHS & INJURIES vs. SEAT BELT USE, 1986–2005

Notice the relationship between increased seat belt use and decreased fatalities and serious injuries. You can apply this information by using a seat belt when you are in a car.

Sometimes you will be asked to predict how someone else would likely apply the information given in a table or graph. Look at the table below.

Rank	Country	Proved Reserves (billion barrels)
GREATEST OIL RESERVES BY COUNTRY 2005		
1	Saudi Arabia	261.9
2	Canada	178.8
3	Iran	125.8
4	Iraq	115.0
5	Kuwait	101.5
6	United Arab Emirates	97.8
7	Venezuela	77.2
8	Russia	60.0
9	Libya	39.0
10	Nigeria	35.3

Source: Oil & Gas Journal, Vol. 102, No. 47 (Dec. 10, 2004).
From U.S Energy Information Administration

1 Saudi Arabia, Iran, Iraq, Kuwait, and the United Arab Emirates are all Middle Eastern countries. Given that information, how do you think the United States government applies the information in the chart?

GED Practice

Question 1 refers to the following graph.

INDUSTRY CONTRIBUTION TO NET
JOB GROWTH, Jan. 2005–Jan. 2006

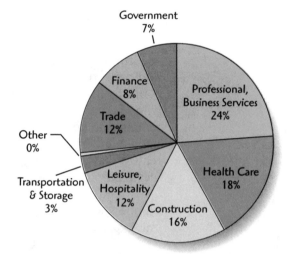

1 If you were unemployed, getting your GED, and entering a job training program, which of the following would offer the fewest new job opportunities?

  ① heavy equipment operator
  ② certified nurse's assistant
  ③ hotel clerk
  ④ truck driver
  ⑤ office assistant

Question 2 is based on the following table.

1998 UNITED STATES UNINTENTIONAL INJURIES AND ADVERSE EFFECTS Ages 15–24, All Races, Both Sexes		
Cause of Death	Number of Deaths	Percentage of Deaths
MV Traffic	9,828	73.6%
Poisoning	860	6.4%
Drowning/Submersion	821	6.2%
Transport, Other	280	2.1%
Firearm	260	1.9%
Fall	226	1.7%
Fire/Burn	195	1.5%
Unspecified	142	1.1%
Pedestrian, Other	136	1.0%
Struck by, against	133	1.0%
Other specified and classifiable	128	1.0%
Suffocation	125	0.9%
Machinery	70	0.5%
Natural/Environmental	68	0.5%
Medical Care, Adverse Effects	41	0.3%
Cut/Pierce	12	0.1%
Drug, Adverse Effects	9	0.1%
Pedal cyclist, other	9	0.1%
Other specified/NEC	4	0.0%
Overexertion	2	0.0%
Total Deaths	**13,349**	

Source: National Center for Health Statistics (NCHS) Vital Statistics System for Numbers of Deaths.

2 Applying the information in this table, what can a young person do to reduce his or her chance of dying as the result of an accident?

  ① Read labels carefully before taking any medications.
  ② Drive defensively and only when necessary.
  ③ Always use a flotation device when in a boat or canoe.
  ④ Never use cigarettes inside a house.
  ⑤ Learn the proper use of machinery before using it.

Recognizing Unstated Assumptions

The data that goes into a table or graph is sometimes obtained on the basis of underlying assumptions, or **unstated assumptions**. It is a good practice to question how valid and accurate some data is. Look at the following graphs. What is an unstated assumption that is made in these graphs?

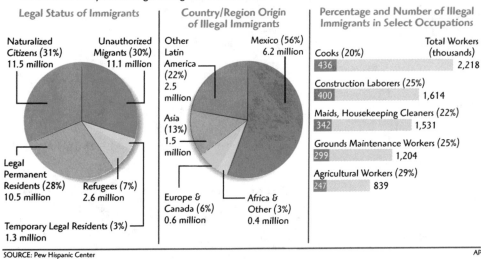

NEARLY ONE-THIRD OF IMMIGRANTS IN UNITED STATES ILLEGALLY

More than 11 million immigrants are not authorized to be in the United States, based on estimates from a 2005 study. Most illegal immigrants are from Mexico or other Latin American countries.

Legal Status of Immigrants

Naturalized Citizens (31%) 11.5 million
Unauthorized Migrants (30%) 11.1 million
Legal Permanent Residents (28%) 10.5 million
Refugees (7%) 2.6 million
Temporary Legal Residents (3%) 1.3 million

Country/Region Origin of Illegal Immigrants

Other Latin America (22%) 2.5 million
Mexico (56%) 6.2 million
Asia (13%) 1.5 million
Europe & Canada (6%) 0.6 million
Africa & Other (3%) 0.4 million

Percentage and Number of Illegal Immigrants in Select Occupations

		Total Workers (thousands)
Cooks (20%)	436	2,218
Construction Laborers (25%)	400	1,614
Maids, Housekeeping Cleaners (22%)	342	1,531
Grounds Maintenance Workers (25%)	299	1,204
Agricultural Workers (29%)	247	839

SOURCE: Pew Hispanic Center   AP

The assumption that is made in these graphs is that there is an accurate and dependable method of counting illegal immigrants, who make every effort to remain undetected and uncounted. You should realize that the numbers for illegal immigrants are not as dependable as the numbers for legal immigrants, who are counted by the U.S. Census Bureau and have no reason to be undetected or uncounted.

Now look at the following graph.

PERCENTAGE OF TEENAGERS WHO HAVE HAD SEXUAL INTERCOURSE AT DIFFERENT AGES, 1995

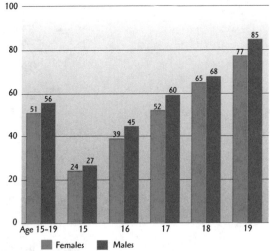

Females | Males

Sources: 1995 National Survey of Family Growth and 1995 National Survey of Adolescent Males

1 What is an unstated assumption of this graph?

GED Practice

Question 1 refers to the following graph.

ESTIMATED ANNUAL DOMESTIC RETAIL-LEVEL DRUG PURCHASES IN BILLIONS OF DOLLARS, 2000

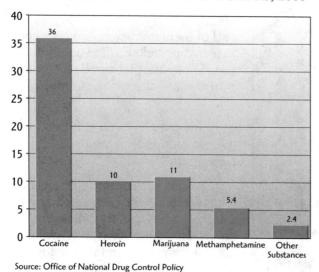

Source: Office of National Drug Control Policy

1 Which of the following is an unstated assumption of the graph?

(1) More money is spent on cocaine than the other illegal drugs.

(2) Marijuana is not as dangerous as the other illegal drugs.

(3) It is possible to get accurate estimates of illegal drug purchases.

(4) The war on drugs is necessary to combat the use of illegal drugs.

(5) The drugs listed are the major illegal drugs used in the U.S.

Question 2 is based on the following graph.

THE MAJOR THREATS TO GLOBALLY THREATENED MAMMAL, AMPHIBIAN, AND BIRD SPECIES

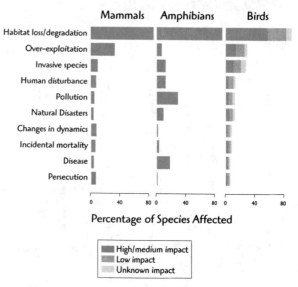

2 Which of the following is an unstated assumption of the graph?

(1) The major threats to these animals are known.

(2) It is possible to figure out what caused a species to disappear.

(3) It is too late to do anything to save threatened animals.

(4) The greatest threat to animals is habitat loss and degradation.

(5) It can be predicted what the future threats to these animals are.

Judging the Adequacy of Facts

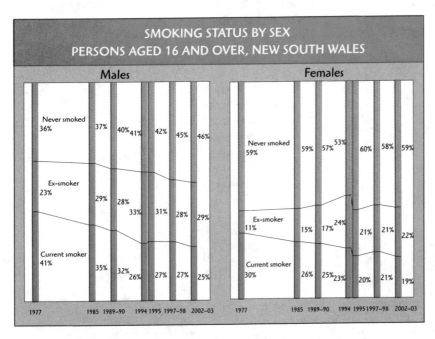

SMOKING STATUS BY SEX
PERSONS AGED 16 AND OVER, NEW SOUTH WALES

Males

Never smoked 36% 37% 40% 41% 42% 45% 46%

Ex-smoker 23% 29% 28% 33% 31% 28% 29%

Current smoker 41% 35% 32% 26% 27% 27% 25%

1977   1985 1989–90 1994 1995 1997–98 2002–03

Females

Never smoked 59% 59% 57% 53% 60% 58% 59%

Ex-smoker 11% 15% 17% 24% 21% 21% 22%

Current smoker 30% 26% 25% 23% 20% 21% 19%

1977   1985 1989–90 1994 1995 1997–98 2002–03

We can use tables and graphs to help us answer questions. Sometimes the information in a table or graph is adequate for us to answer our question. Other times, it only provides part of the information we need. Look at the graph below. Can you think of a question to ask that can be answered by the information in the graph?

One question that can be answered with this data is: Is there a trend in the percentage of current smokers in New South Wales?

Now look at this similar question: Is there a trend in the number of current smokers in New South Wales? You do not have adequate facts to answer this question. You need to know the total number of males and females for each of the years that have percentage data.

On March 23, 2006, ABC published a poll, shown at the left, which ranked the leading Republican and Democratic presidential candidates. The ranking reflected the chance of each person to get the nomination of their party, not their chance of winning in 2008.

For each question, decide whether or not there is adequate information in the table. If there is adequate information, write A and answer the question. If there is not adequate information, write N and the additional information needed.

ABC VOTE 2008: INVISIBLE PRIMARY RATINGS
(The closer the rating is to 1.0, the better chance of securing the nomination.)

Potential Republican Candidates		Potential Democrat Candidates	
John McCain	1.42	Hillary Clinton	1.74
George Allen	3.58	John Edwards	2.89
Mitt Romney	4.05	Mark Warner	4.00
Rudy Giuliani	4.63	John Kerry	5.68
Mike Huckabee	5.53	Tom Vilsack	5.95
Newt Gingrich	6.11	Evan Bayh	5.95
Bill Frist	6.16	Bill Richardson	6.58
George Pataki	7.00	Joe Biden	6.68
Chuck Hagel	7.89	Wesley Clark	7.47
Sam Brownback	8.26	Tom Daschle	7.63
Tom Tancredo	10.58	Russ Feingold	8.42

❶ Who will win the 2008 presidential nomination for the Republicans?

_____

❷ Who is the leading candidate for the Democrats?

_____

GED Practice

Question 1 refers to the following graph.

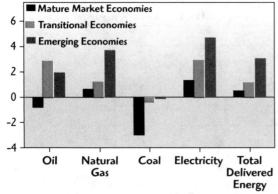

GROWTH IN RESIDENTIAL FUEL CONSUMPTION, 2002–2025
AVERAGE ANNUAL PERCENT CHANGE

- ■ Mature Market Economies
- ■ Transitional Economies
- ■ Emerging Economies

Source: Energy Information Administration (EIA).

1 Which of the following questions cannot be answered using the information from the graph?

  ① Which type of economy is expected to have the greatest increase in energy consumption by 2025?

  ② Which type of energy will experience the most rapid rate of consumption growth by 2025?

  ③ Which type of energy is expected to have the greatest decrease in consumption by 2025?

  ④ Is oil consumption in the mature market economies expected to increase or decrease by 2025?

  ⑤ Which type of fuel provides the most energy consumed by the transitional economies?

Question 2 is based on the following table.

Rank	Country	Personal Computers (per 1,000 population)	Year
	PERSONAL COMPUTERS BY COUNTRY (per 1,000 population)		
1	Switzerland	709.1	2002
2	United States	658.4	2002
3	Sweden	622.5	2002
4	Singapore	620.9	2002
5	Luxembourg	592.8	2002
6	Denmark	576.5	2002
7	Australia	564.8	2002
8	Korea, South	555.4	2002
9	Norway	529.7	2002
10	Bermuda	506.0	2001

2 Which of the following questions can be answered using the information from the above graph?

  ① How many personal computers per 1,000 people were there in Sweden in 2002?

  ② How many personal computers were there in use in Switzerland in 2002?

  ③ What country will have the greatest number of computers per 1,000 people in 2010?

  ④ What country has the fastest growing number of personal computers per 1,000 people?

  ⑤ How many personal computers are sold per year in the United States?

Identifying Cause and Effect Relationships

Tables and graphs can be used to show **cause and effect relationships**. What cause and effect relationship is the following graph trying to illustrate?

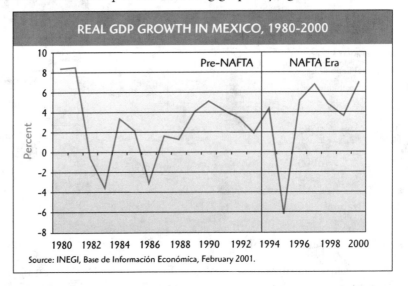

REAL GDP GROWTH IN MEXICO, 1980-2000

Source: INEGI, Base de Información Económica, February 2001.

The graph is illustrating the cause and effect relationship between NAFTA (North American Free Trade Agreement) and GDP (gross domestic product) growth in Mexico. Before it was passed, NAFTA had been touted as a program that would bring prosperity to Mexico. The graph shows that this effect did not happen. Instead, there was a sharp decline in GDP in 1995, after NAFTA began. Despite better numbers later in the 1990s, GDP growth still had not matched the pre-NAFTA levels of the early 1980s.

The following table contains information on HIV/AIDS in sub-Saharan Africa. Just those nations in the region with the highest numbers of HIV/AIDS cases are listed.

SUB-SAHARAN AFRICA				
HIV and AIDS statistics and features in 2003 and 2005				
	Adults and children living with HIV	Number of women living with HIV	Adults and children newly infected with HIV	Adult prevalence (%)*	Adult and child deaths due to AIDS
2005	25.8 million [23.8–28.9 million]	13.5 million [12.5–15.1 million]	3.2 million [2.8–3.9 million]	7.2 [6.6–8.0]	2.4 million [2.1–2.7 million]
2003	24.9 million [23.0–27.9 million]	13.1 million [12.1–14.6 million]	3.0 million [2.7–3.7 million]	7.3 [6.7–8.1]	2.1 million [1.9–2.4 million]

SOURCE: AIDS epidemic update: December 2005

❶ What cause and effect relationship is documented in this table?

GED Practice

Question 1 refers to the following graph.

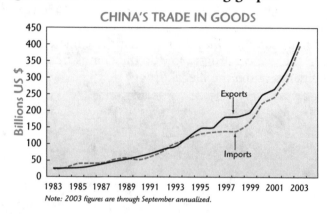

CHINA'S TRADE IN GOODS

Note: 2003 figures are through September annualized.

1 What would be the most likely effect of the trend shown in this graph of China's trade in goods from 1983 to 2003?

  ① China will become increasingly isolated from the rest of the world.

  ② China will take action to decrease imports from other countries.

  ③ The Chinese people will be resistant to changes in the economy.

  ④ China will have a greater impact on the economies of other nations.

  ⑤ China will move toward establishing a more democratic government.

Question 2 is based on the following graph of Major League Baseball financial data.

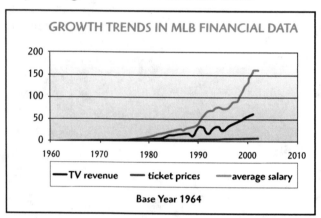

GROWTH TRENDS IN MLB FINANCIAL DATA

— TV revenue — ticket prices — average salary

Base Year 1964

2 Which of the following most likely describes a cause and effect relationship that is supported by data from the above graph?

  ① Increased salaries are a cause of higher ticket prices.

  ② Increased TV revenue helped cause an increase in salaries.

  ③ Higher ticket prices allowed player salaries to increase.

  ④ TV revenues helped increase the value of MLB teams.

  ⑤ Increased TV revenues helped cause higher ticket prices.

Identifying Comparisons and Contrasts

Tables and graphs can clearly illustrate **comparisons** and **contrasts**. The following graph shows annual drug deaths in the United States. Tobacco and alcohol are legal for adults to purchase. Prescription drugs can only be legally bought with a prescription. Cocaine, heroin, and marijuana are illegal drugs that the United States spends billions of dollars to fight in the war on drugs. How do the deaths from the legal substances compare with the deaths from the illegal drugs?

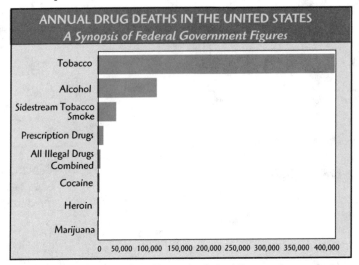

Source: National Institute on Drug Abuse, other Federal Government sources

Far more deaths are the result of the use of legal drugs, especially tobacco and alcohol.

China is considered to have one of the most rapidly growing economies in the world. The following table compares gross national product (GNP) per person in China to the United States.

❶ According to this table, how does gross national product per person in China compare to that of the United States?

_____

_____

_____

CHINA AND THE UNITED STATES GNP PER CAPITA IN NOMINAL U.S. $		
Year(s)	China	United States
1965	85	3,240
1970	160	4,760
1975	380	7,120
1980	270	11,590
1985	310	16,400
1990	370	21,810
1991	370	22,340
1992	380	23,830
1993	490	24,750
1994	530	25,860
1995	620	26,980
1996	750	28,020
1997	860	29,080
1998	750	29,240
1999	780	31,910
2000	840	34,100
2001	890	34,280

GED Practice

Questions 1 and 2 refer to the following table.

American War Troop Casualties								
		Casualties				Percentages		
		Deaths						
Conflict	Enrolled	Combat	Other	Wounded	Total	KIA	Dead	Casualty
Revolutionary War	200.0	4,435	*	6,188	10,623	2.2%	2.2%	5.3%
War of 1812	286.0	2,260	*	4,505	6,765	0.8%	0.8%	2.4%
Mexican War	78.7	1,733	11,550	4,152	17,435	2.2%	16.9%	22.2%
Civil War: Union	2,803.3	110,070	249,458	275,175	634,703	3.9%	12.8%	22.6%
Confederate	1,064.2	74,524	124,000	137,000	335,524 +	7.0%	18.7%	31.5%
Combined	3,867.5	184,594	373,458	412,175	970,227	4.8%	14.4%	25.1%
Spanish-American War	306.8	385	2,061	1,662	4,108	0.1%	0.8%	1.3%
World War I	4,743.8	53,513	63,195	204,002	320,710	1.1%	2.5%	6.8%
World War II	16,353.7	292,131	115,185	670,846	1,078,162	1.8%	2.5%	6.6%
Korean War	5,764.1	33,651	*	103,284	136,935	0.6%	0.6%	2.4%
Vietnam War	8,744.0	47,369	10,799	153,303	211,471	0.5%	0.7%	2.4%
Gulf War	2,750.0	148	145	467	760	0.0%	0.0%	0.0%

* Non–battle deaths not known for these wars.
+ Confederate non–battle deaths and wounded estimated.

1 According to the table, the war that resulted in the greatest percentage of Americans killed in action was

- (1) Revolutionary War
- (2) Civil War
- (3) World War I
- (4) World War II
- (5) Vietnam War

2 According to the table, the war that had the greatest number of Americans enrolled in the military was

- (1) Revolutionary War
- (2) Civil War
- (3) World War I
- (4) World War II
- (5) Vietnam War

Questions 3 and 4 are based on the following graph.

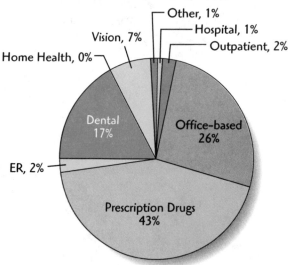

DISTRIBUTION OF OUT-OF-POCKET SPENDING FOR AVERAGE PERSON FOR MEDICAL EXPENSES, 2003

- Other, 1%
- Hospital, 1%
- Outpatient, 2%
- Vision, 7%
- Home Health, 0%
- Dental 17%
- Office-based 26%
- ER, 2%
- Prescription Drugs 43%

3 According to the graph, the single largest type of out-of-pocket medical expense for the average person is

- (1) emergency room
- (2) dental
- (3) vision
- (4) office-based
- (5) prescription drugs

4 According to the graph, how much more is spent out-of-pocket for office-based care as compared with emergency room care?

- (1) 15%
- (2) 24%
- (3) 28%
- (4) 41%
- (5) 43%

Recognizing Values

We all have **values,** or things that are most important to us. Nations can have values as well. It might be devotion to democracy or patriotism, or the economic well-being of its citizens. It might also be the well-being of its powerful leaders and most influential companies. Tables and graphs can clarify the values of an individual, group, or nation by illustrating choices and priorities. The following chart shows the level of infant mortality in the United States from 1950 to 2000. What does this chart say about the importance of infant survival in the United States?

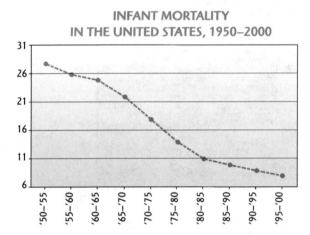

INFANT MORTALITY
IN THE UNITED STATES, 1950–2000

The graph can be considered evidence that Americans value the survival of infants.

The following graph shows the change in the distribution of wealth in the United States from 1983 to 1998.

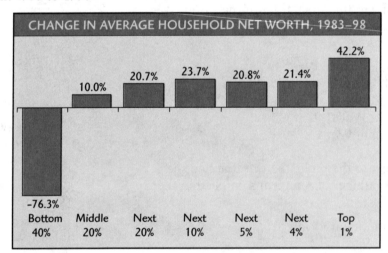

CHANGE IN AVERAGE HOUSEHOLD NET WORTH, 1983–98

❶ What does this graph say about values in the United States?

GED Practice

Questions 1 and 2 refer to the following graph.

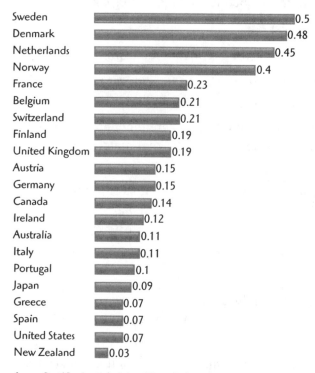

QUALITY-ADJUSTED AID AND CHARITABLE GIVING/GDP(%)

Sweden	0.5
Denmark	0.48
Netherlands	0.45
Norway	0.4
France	0.23
Belgium	0.21
Switzerland	0.21
Finland	0.19
United Kingdom	0.19
Austria	0.15
Germany	0.15
Canada	0.14
Ireland	0.12
Australia	0.11
Italy	0.11
Portugal	0.1
Japan	0.09
Greece	0.07
Spain	0.07
United States	0.07
New Zealand	0.03

Source: David Roodman, *An Index of Donor Performance*, Center for Global Development, April 2004

1 In 1970, the richest nations of the world pledged to devote 0.7 percent of gross domestic product (GDP) to foreign aid. According to the chart, how many nations honored their pledges?

(1) no nations
(2) 1 nation
(3) 4 nations
(4) 20 nations
(5) 21 nations

2 Which nation most showed that it valued helping poor nations?

(1) Sweden
(2) Denmark
(3) France
(4) United States
(5) New Zealand

Questions 3 and 4 are based on the following table.

DEFORESTATION AND REFORESTATION RATES, SELECTED ASIA-PACIFIC COUNTRIES, 1990. (1,000 Ha)				
Region/Country	Annual Deforestation	Annual Reforestation	Total Forest Plantations	Other Wooded Lands
SOUTH ASIA				
Bangladesh	38	12.3	235	468
Bhutan	16	0.2	4	355
India	339	1,009.0	13,320	17,689
Nepal	54	4.3	56	672
Pakistan	77	4.2	168	1,105
Sri Lanka	27	6.0	139	2,113
SOUTHEAST ASIA				
Cambodia	131	331.8	7	1,554
Indonesia	1,212	0.1	6,125	29,434
Laos	129		4	8,259
Malaysia	396	6.3	81	4,584
Myanmar	401	19.6	235	20,683
Philippines	316		203	5,606
Thailand	515	29.4	529	1,704
Vietnam	137	49.0	49	13,171
EAST ASIA				
Mongolia	60			4,335
SOUTH PACIFIC				
Fiji	4	5.0	78	6
Papua New Guinea	113	1.5	30	6,085
Solomons	5	0.3	16	45
Vanuatu	8	0.4	7	0
Western Samoa	2	0.5	9	31

Source: National Forestry Action Programmes, Update No. 32, July 1995, FAO, Rome.

3 According to information in the table, India appears to value

(1) economic growth
(2) forest exploitation
(3) conservation
(4) developing industry
(5) preserving wildlife

4 The nation that appears to value maximizing forest exploitation is

(1) Bangladesh
(2) Sri Lanka
(3) Cambodia
(4) Indonesia
(5) Fiji

Taking the GED Test

Congratulations on completing the instruction section of *Top 50 Social Studies Skills for GED Success*. You are now familiar with the types and difficulty levels of questions you will see on the GED Social Studies Test. As you ready yourself for the GED Social Studies Test, you may want to think about these good test-taking strategies:

- Get a good night's sleep before the test.

- Eat breakfast before the test, especially if you are taking the test in the morning.

- Arrive at the testing center a few minutes early. If you have never been to the testing center, visit it before the day of the test so you can find it easily.

- Read the test directions carefully. Read each question carefully and be sure you understand what is being asked. Then select the answer that matches each question.

- Grid your answers carefully, ensuring that you mark each answer in the place provided for it. If you erase an answer, be sure you erase it completely.

- If you are not sure of an answer, make an educated guess. When you leave a question unanswered, you will always lose a point, but you may gain the point if you make a correct guess.

- During the test, work quickly and accurately. If you do not know the answer to a question, try to eliminate any options that do not make sense and select the best answer from the remaining options.

- All questions on the test have the same point value. Because of this, make sure you answer all of the easier questions. In other words, don't spend a lot of time on a more difficult question. If you find yourself spending a lot of time on a single question, stop working on that item. Put a question mark beside the question number or write the number on your scratch paper. Then mark the answer you think is most likely correct, and go on to the next question. If you have time at the end of the test, go back to the difficult questions and check your answers.

- If you find yourself feeling nervous or unable to focus, close your eyes for a moment or two and take a few deep breaths. Then return to the test.

About the GED Posttest

This GED Posttest is a review of the 50 skills presented in this book. It is parallel in form to the Pretest you took at the beginning of this book. It will demonstrate what you have learned from the specific skills you practiced throughout this book and will identify any areas you need to review before taking the GED Social Studies Test.

Take this test just as you would the GED Test. On the GED Test, you will have 70 minutes to read the passages, graphs, maps, photographs, cartoons, tables, and charts and complete the 50 questions. For best practice, allow yourself 70 minutes to complete the Posttest in this book.

Answer every question on this Posttest. When time is up, mark the questions you did not finish. Then take extra time to answer those questions, too. That will give you an idea of how much faster you need to work on the actual test.

After you finish, turn to the Answer Key on page 159 to check your answers. Then use the GED Posttest Evaluation Chart (pages 142–143) to figure out which skills to review in the instruction section of this book. You may also use the pages from Contemporary's *GED Social Studies* for further practice and review.

GED Posttest

Questions 1 and 2 refer to the following passage.

The dot-com companies were very successful from 1997 to 2001. During that time, many new Internet start-up companies sprang up. Young, bright entrepreneurs came up with new business models using the potential of the World Wide Web. Investors poured money into these companies. When these new companies made public offerings of stock, the public eagerly bought shares. Many of these entrepreneurs became instant millionaires without their companies ever earning a profit.

A common business model of the dot-com era was to focus on name recognition over making money. Companies would give away items or services either for free or at a loss in order to ensure that the public knew who they were. The object was to build market share, no matter what the cost. Many companies were following this model, and it was inevitable that most of them would fail.

When the end came, it came hard. After stock values peaked in March 2000, they started declining quickly. The fortunes that had appeared so suddenly disappeared just as quickly. As many of the dot-com companies used up the money they had raised from investors and the stock market, they went out of business. Except for a few survivors, most of the dot-coms collapsed and disappeared.

1 The main idea of this passage is

(1) the dot-coms were exciting companies to work for

(2) risk takers can easily make a fortune with dot-coms

(3) it is wise to be cautious about investing in a new fad

(4) the Internet made possible a new way of doing business

(5) during the period from 1997 to 2001, many dot-coms made and lost fortunes

2 Which of the following historical events was similar to the dot-coms?

(1) During the Age of Discovery, European nations raced to control most of the rest of the world. These empires lasted for as long as hundreds of years.

(2) In the 1630s, tulip mania gripped Holland. People spent their entire life savings for a single bulb. In 1637, the tulip market collapsed, bankrupting thousands.

(3) In the early 1800s, New England farmers abandoned their rocky farms for the better soils of the Midwest. The Midwest farm belt is still productive today.

(4) After the invention of the printing press by Gutenberg in 1440, the production and printing of books grew rapidly. As a result, many people learned to read.

(5) Starting in 1982, the stock market moved upward, with some periodic downturns, for 20 years. Despite losses since then, a 1980 investor would still be ahead.

Questions 3 and 4 refer to the following passage.

The Taliban were ultraconservative Islamic fundamentalists who controlled most of Afghanistan from 1994 to 2001. *Taliban* means "student" in Persian. The Taliban leaders had attended schools in Pakistan called *madrassas*. These madrassas taught an extreme form of Islam. After the Soviet withdrawal from Afghanistan, the Taliban, with support from Pakistan, quickly became the leading power. At first, they were popular with the Afghan people because they were seen as honest and incorruptible. They were also fierce fighters.

Once they occupied the capital of Kabul and controlled most of the country, they enforced many extreme policies. Women lost virtually all their rights, including the right to go to school and go out in public alone. The government adopted Shari'ah, the fundamentalist Islamic law. It included punishments such as amputation of a hand for theft and stoning for adultery. Television, music, and sports were all banned. Much of the cultural heritage of Afghanistan, especially its Buddhist monuments, was systematically destroyed. The Taliban, who were Pashtun, the largest ethnic group in the country, oppressed minority groups. In particular, many of the Hazaras minority were persecuted and killed, and their women were enslaved.

The Taliban also provided a safe haven for the Islamic terrorists al-Qaeda, led by Osama bin Laden. With Taliban protection, they were able to set up training camps for terrorists who were dispatched around the world. After the attacks on the World Trade Center and the Pentagon on September 11, 2001, the United States led an invasion of Afghanistan that ended the Taliban reign of terror.

3 The type of government Afghanistan had under the Taliban can best be described as a(n)

① democracy
② monarchy
③ theocracy
④ dictatorship
⑤ oligarchy

4 A value that the Taliban believed in was

① tolerance
② human rights
③ multiculturalism
④ rule by law
⑤ compassion

Questions 5 and 6 refer to the following passage.

Every part of this soil is sacred in the estimation of my people. Every hillside, every valley, every plain and grove, has been hallowed by some sad or happy event in days long vanished. Even the rocks, which seem to be dumb and dead as the swelter in the sun along the silent shore, thrill with memories of stirring events connected with the lives of my people, and the very dust upon which you now stand responds more lovingly to their footsteps than yours, because it is rich with the blood of our ancestors, and our bare feet are conscious of the sympathetic touch. Our departed braves, fond mothers, glad, happy hearted maidens, and even the little children who lived here and rejoiced here for a brief season, will love these somber solitudes and at eventide they greet shadowy returning spirits. And when the last Red Man shall have perished, and the memory of my tribe shall have become a myth among the White Men, these shores will swarm with the invisible dead of my tribe, and when your children's children think themselves alone in the field, the store, the shop, upon the highway, or in the silence of the pathless woods, they will not be alone. In all the earth there is no place dedicated to solitude. At night when the streets of your cities and villages are silent and you think them deserted, they will throng with the returning hosts that once filled them and still love this beautiful land. The White Man will never be alone.

—Chief Seattle, 1854

5 What was Chief Seattle trying to explain?

① No matter the price, his tribe will never willingly leave its land.
② His people and the land are bound together through love.
③ He expects his people to regain the land when the White Man leaves.
④ His people will want to visit their sacred places at night.
⑤ It is possible for Red Men and White Men to live together in peace.

6 What is an important difference in the way that Chief Seattle and the American government view the land?

① Chief Seattle believed that living on the land creates an eternal connection to it, while the American government believed land could be bought and sold.
② Chief Seattle believed that his people were going to die out, while the American government believed that they would survive.
③ Chief Seattle was willing to have his people live with the White Man, while the American government did not want settlers living with the Indians.
④ Chief Seattle wanted his people to control the land, while the American government wanted its people to control the land.
⑤ Chief Seattle thought that the land was priceless, while the American government did not believe that the land had much value.

Questions 7 and 8 refer to the following passage.

People create a social movement to challenge established power. They identify responsibility for their discontent and focus their energy toward social change. A movement can change a political system or it can challenge cultural values.

While there have been movements throughout American history, the 1960s and early 1970s were the most active period. The civil rights movement, the environmental movement, the peace movement, the gay rights movement, the migrant farm worker movement, and the women's movement all flourished during this period. The passing of historic civil rights legislation and the murder of Martin Luther King made the civil rights movement less urgent and less focused. The end of the Vietnam War also marked the end of the peace movement. The mass entry of women into the workforce and the advancement of some women seemed to dampen the women's movement.

Today, there are still movements of the right and left. Some of the movements of the 1960s have evolved and refocused. New movements have formed, such as an immigrants' rights movement and an anti-Iraq War movement. As long as we have an American democracy, we will have social movements trying to influence it.

7 What is implied in the idea that we will always have social movements?

  ① If we work hard enough, we can have a just society that satisfies everybody.
  ② Americans looking for some group to join will always have a good selection.
  ③ There are no perfect political solutions that work forever and satisfy everybody.
  ④ Americans are spoiled malcontents who are never satisfied with what they have.
  ⑤ Political institutions need to reform their power structure to accept opposing ideas.

8 During the 1960s and 1970s, the Baby Boom Generation was coming of age. Why might this have had an impact on the social movements of the time?

  ① There were many people who did not remember the fight against fascism.
  ② They missed the Great Depression and grew up with more material goods.
  ③ They were the first generation to grow up with television.
  ④ People coming of age are most likely to become activists.
  ⑤ They were the first suburban generation and expected privileges.

Questions 9 and 10 refer to the following passage.

The Industrial Revolution was one of the great changes in human history. An economy that was based on manual labor was replaced by an economy based on machinery. Although the Industrial Revolution began in the textile industry, it soon spread to other areas. There were many innovations that contributed to the Industrial Revolution, but a key one was the invention of the steam engine in England. Machinery powered by steam led to huge productivity increases. The factory system led to an even greater increase in productivity. Steam engines were also adapted for transportation. The steam locomotive and the steamboat transformed transportation.

In the end, the Industrial Revolution was more about innovation, invention, and change than it was about any one invention or change. Many of the inventions, processes, and materials of the Industrial Revolution are now outdated. But the search for improved productivity and better products that began with the Industrial Revolution continues to this day.

9 An unstated assumption in this passage is

① the Industrial Revolution was a positive event for humanity
② it is better to use machinery than muscle power in many industries
③ a key component of the Industrial Revolution was innovation
④ preindustrial life had advantages that are now all but forgotten
⑤ every country started the Industrial Revolution with steam engines

10 From the information in this passage, it is reasonable to conclude that

① many nations do not want the economy to move from manual labor to machinery
② the Industrial Revolution did not have to start with textiles and steam
③ the Industrial Revolution directly led to the development of democracy
④ the Industrial Revolution created as many problems as it solved
⑤ the Industrial Revolution improved the lives of everyone

Questions 11 and 12 refer to the following passage.

The Israeli-Palestinian conflict has persisted for more than half a century. Both sides have strong claims to the land and strong grievances against each other. To Jewish Israelis, Israel is their ancient homeland. Their ancestors were exiled from Israel nearly two thousand years ago by the Romans. For all that time, Jews did not give up the hope of returning to the land of Israel.

However, during that time, the land did not remain vacant. The Romans renamed the area Palestine. The current Arab residents of the West Bank and Gaza consider themselves to be Palestinians. They believe that Palestine includes all of Israel, as well as the West Bank and Gaza. They believe that Palestinians who were driven from their land during the Israeli War of Independence should be allowed to return.

Most Jewish Israelis oppose a Palestinian right of return. They fear that they could become a minority in Israel if millions of Palestinians are allowed to return. In addition, hundreds of thousands of Jews migrated from Islamic countries to Israel in the years following Israeli independence. They were fleeing persecution and hoping for a better life in Israel.

Militant Palestinians believe that any means is justified while fighting their occupation by Israel. The suicide bomber who blows himself up with explosives wrapped around him and who tries to kill as many people as possible is seen by the militants as a martyr. To the Israelis, he is a vicious terrorist out to kill and injure innocent people.

Palestinians are angry about the occupation of the West Bank and Gaza by Israeli forces. They are humiliated by their treatment at the hands of the Israelis.

On the other hand, Israelis fear for their safety and go to great lengths to stop suicide bombers and other attackers from entering Israel. They are building a wall to separate Israel from the West Bank. They are also severely restricting access to Israel by Palestinian workers.

With grievances so deep and passions so high, there does not appear to be any solution for this never-ending conflict. Both sides need to be ready to make hard compromises in order to reach a peace agreement. And if a peace agreement is actually reached, then the daunting work can begin of healing the wounds of decades of conflict.

11 In what way are the Palestinian and Israeli viewpoints similar?

① They believe that Jews and Muslims should be able to live together.
② They are most concerned about the threats to their security.
③ They both want to rule all the people of Israel and Palestine.
④ They both believe that they have the more valid grievances.
⑤ They both believe that any action for their cause is justified.

12 There are adequate facts in this passage to determine that

① the Palestinian viewpoint of the conflict is the valid one
② the Israeli viewpoint of the conflict is the valid one
③ there are simple solutions to the Israeli-Palestinian conflict
④ great courage will be needed to solve this conflict
⑤ there is no possible peaceful solution for this conflict

Questions 13 and 14 refer to the following passage.

Medieval towns offered their residents some independence from feudal rule. But life in the towns was still highly controlled, usually organized around guilds, which were similar to trade unions. Guilds controlled all commerce and trade in the medieval town. There were guilds for merchants and guilds for skilled craftsmen. Each guild regulated the number of apprentices and workmen, the hours of labor, the wages, and the quality of products. They also helped their own needy members, including widows and orphans. By controlling prices and maintaining standards for products, they helped maintain customers' trust and confidence. However, they could also become overly rigid and resist any innovation or change. As a result, as the medieval period came to a close and the pace of change quickened, guilds were unable to keep up with that change and began to disappear.

13 Which of the following is an opinion?

① Craft guilds offered customers quality control for products.
② If a guild member died, his wife and children were helped by the guild.
③ Guilds could have adjusted to change if they realized they had to.
④ Prices for products were set by the craft guild who made them.
⑤ The way to learn a craft in a medieval town was to become an apprentice.

14 All of the following were causes of the success of medieval guilds except

① guaranteed prices
② quality control
③ stability and consistency
④ a dependable training system
⑤ new techniques and technology

Questions 15 and 16 refer to the following passage.

There has been another murder committed within a few miles of this place, which has given us something to gossip about, for the committee of vigilance had the good nature, purely for our amusement I conclude, to apprehend a lucky individual (I call him lucky advisedly, for he had all his expenses paid at the Humboldt, was remunerated for his lost time, enjoyed a holiday from hard work, had a sort of guard of honor composed of the most respectable men on the river, and was of more consequence for four days than ever he had been in the whole of his insignificant little life before) whom somebody fancied bore a faint resemblance to the description of the murderer.
—Mrs. Louise Amelia Knapp Smith Clappe,
1851, California

15 What is Louise Clappe's point of view about the murder?

① She treats it lightly as an ordinary occurrence.
② She is completely devastated and grief stricken.
③ She is obsessed with finding the real murderer.
④ She is concerned for her own safety.
⑤ She is very respectful of the work of law enforcement.

16 There is enough information in this letter to determine that

① it was very unusual to have a murder in the area
② Louise Clappe was a very sensitive and compassionate person
③ the committee of vigilance wanted to entertain Mrs. Clappe
④ in order to get out of work, men tried to get arrested
⑤ the man who had been arrested for the murder was innocent

Questions 17 and 18 refer to the following passage.

The Sudanese government, using Arab "Janjaweed" militias, its air force, and organized starvation, is systematically killing the black Sudanese of Darfur. Over two and a half million people, driven from their homes, now face death from starvation and disease as the Sudanese government and Janjaweed militias attempt to prevent humanitarian aid from reaching them. The same forces have destroyed the people of Darfur's villages and crops. They have poisoned their water supplies, and they continue to murder, rape, and terrorize. The Sudanese government, while publicly denying that it supports the Janjaweed, is providing arms and assistance and has participated in joint attacks with the group.

The conflict began in February 2003. There are estimates that more than 300,000 people have already died. Two hundred thousand more have fled to neighboring Chad. The Darfur conflict has been described by mass media as ethnic cleansing and genocide.

Even though the media implies that this genocide is racially motivated, both sides are largely black in skin tone. The distinction between "Arab" and "non-Arab," common in Western media, is heavily disputed by many people, including the Sudanese government. It might be more helpful to understand the conflict as a competition between farmers and nomadic cattle herders who compete for scarce resources. It is clear, however, that the targeting of ethnic groups who are subsistence farmers has caused various crimes against humanity. Many of these fall under the category of genocide, according to international law.

17 Many errors in reasoning are pointed out in the article. Which of the following shows good reasoning?

(1) It is an oversimplification to see the conflict as caused by skin color.
(2) Violence should be used to resolve a conflict between farmers and herders.
(3) The Sudanese government is innocent because it claims to be.
(4) Genocide is an acceptable method of resolving a conflict.
(5) The actions of the Janjaweed militias are a crime against humanity.

18 Which of the following cannot be used to persuade the reader to oppose the actions of the Sudanese government?

(1) Two and a half million people have been driven from their homes.
(2) The Sudanese government is trying to hinder the flow of aid to refugees.
(3) Villages and crops have been destroyed and water supplies poisoned.
(4) The Arab Sudanese government is in conflict with non-Arabs in Darfur.
(5) More than 300,000 have died in Darfur from murder, starvation, or disease.

Questions 19 and 20 refer to the following map.

MILITARY GOVERNMENTS 1945 TO 1995

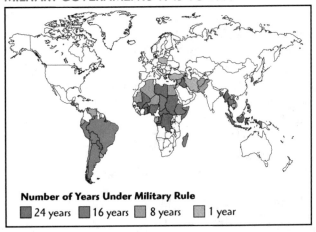

Number of Years Under Military Rule
◼ 24 years ◼ 16 years ◼ 8 years ◻ 1 year

19 According to the map, which of these areas of the world were under military rule for more than twenty-four years?

① the United States
② Northern and Central Africa
③ Southern Africa
④ Russia
⑤ South America

20 None of the leading industrialized nations of the world were under military rule from 1945 to 1995. You can apply that information and the information on the map to determine that

① none of the countries in Europe were industrialized at that time
② the Republic of the Congo in Central Africa was not industrialized
③ Brazil, the largest nation of South America, was industrialized
④ the United States was the world's leading industrialized nation
⑤ Northern Africa has great potential for industrial growth

Questions 21 and 22 refer to the following map.

POPULATION DENSITY—2000

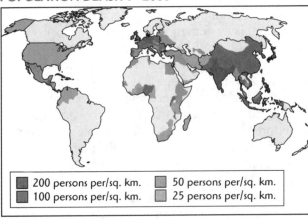

◼ 200 persons per/sq. km. ◼ 50 persons per/sq. km.
◼ 100 persons per/sq. km. ◻ 25 persons per/sq. km.

21 A conclusion that you can draw from this map is

① the earth has room for population growth
② the earth is dangerously overcrowded
③ China is the most densely populated nation
④ South America is overpopulated
⑤ Europe has a reasonable level of population

22 The facts on this map are adequate to determine that

① population growth throughout the world should be encouraged
② India has more than 200 persons per square kilometer
③ South America is experiencing rapid population growth
④ the population of the United States has stabilized
⑤ much of Australia is inhospitable desert

Questions 23 and 24 refer to the following map.

**GADSDEN PURCHASE &
PROPOSED RAIL ROUTES: 1853**

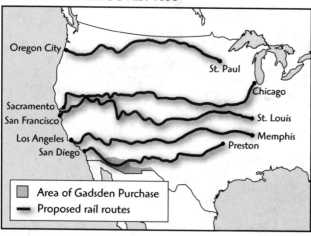

23 What is the key point of this map?

① Many rail routes across the West were proposed.
② A railroad line needed to have its start and end in a large city.
③ The Gadsden Purchase was needed for the southern rail route.
④ Mexico and Canada had no plans for a transcontinental railroad.
⑤ The railroads encouraged westward expansion in the United States.

24 Which of the following is an implication of this map?

① The Gadsden Purchase was obtained purely for economic reasons.
② The desire of New Mexico and Arizona to expand led to the Gadsden Purchase.
③ Competition on competing rail lines helped keep cross country travel affordable.
④ Mexico had little interest in economic development or other progress.
⑤ Mexico was forced into giving up its territory to the United States.

Questions 25 and 26 refer to the following map.

SLAVE CROPS IN THE AMERICAN SOUTH—1860

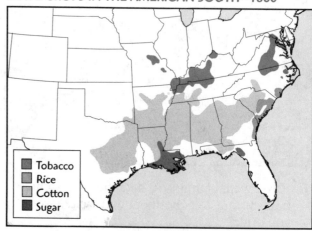

Tobacco
Rice
Cotton
Sugar

25 The purpose of this map is to show

① how the South was dependent on slave labor for its economy
② that agriculture was the dominant economic activity in the South
③ that the end of slavery would bring financial ruin to the South
④ the importance of tobacco to the economy of the South
⑤ why Southerners thought that abolitionists hated the South

26 Which of the following is a fact proven by the above map?

① The South was justified in opposing the abolition of slavery.
② Of the crops raised by slaves, cotton was the most extensively grown.
③ Tobacco was a more economically important crop than cotton.
④ Slaves in 1860 were better farm laborers than migrant workers are today.
⑤ The American South is the best place in the world to grow cotton.

Question 27 refers to the following map.

APPALACHIAN TRAIL

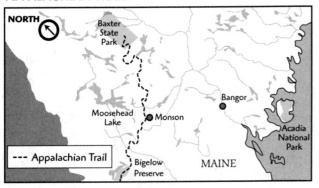

27 If you were planning to hike the Appalachian trail starting at its northern end, where would you drive?

① Bigelow Preserve
② Monson
③ Bangor
④ Acadia National Park
⑤ Baxter State Park

Questions 28 and 29 refer to the following historical cartoon.

"Now, this complete, all-in-one model has a thirty-nine-tube television receiver, equippped for both black-and-white and color reception; AM and FM radio; a record-player geared for 33 1/3 r.p.m., 45 r.p.m., and 78 r.p.m; automatic record-changer; the latest thing in a wire recorder; and this large, roomy cabinet at the bottom, in case anything new is invented."

28 The sign "new line for 1950" shows us when this cartoon was created. If the sign was not there, which of the following would not date this cartoon to the 1950s?

① the size and shape of the television screen
② the television described as having thirty-nine tubes
③ the record player having a 78 r.p.m. setting
④ the absence of a CD or DVD player
⑤ all the electronics together in a media center

29 Which of the following is the best description of this cartoonist's point of view?

① It is a good idea to purchase all forms of home entertainment.
② It is unlikely that any other forms of home entertainment will be invented.
③ Spend as much money as you possibly can for entertainment.
④ A good salesman can sell customers more than they really need.
⑤ Many new forms of home entertainment will be invented.

Question 30 refers to the following cartoon.

30 What unstated assumption is the source of the humor of this cartoon?

① The Town of Hillsville does not have any hills.

② A column of numbers is supposed to be added.

③ A town founded in 1802 should have older homes.

④ The population is small for such a large sign.

⑤ It is important for everyone to know their math facts.

Questions 31 and 32 refer to the following cartoon.

"It's an amazing coincidence, isn't it, that we all served on the same board of directors?"

31 What is this cartoon trying to tell us?

① Older men enjoy having conversations while in a hot tub.

② Even well-meaning corporate board members can end up in hell.

③ Dishonest corporate leaders will pay for their behavior.

④ Wealthy board members need armed guards to protect them.

⑤ You never know where you will meet your co-workers.

32 What is the idea that the cartoonist expects the reader to know and apply?

① Most corporate boards are dominated by old white men.

② People who live a moral life can expect to go to heaven.

③ Corporate leaders like to take vacations in exotic places.

④ After death, a religious person will experience eternal life.

⑤ Hell is a hot place ruled by the devil and occupied by sinners.

Questions 33 and 34 refer to the following political cartoon.

33 What is the main idea of the above cartoon?

① The education system is failing.
② Students do not work hard enough.
③ Maps need to display Louisiana better.
④ Louisiana is soon going to be under water.
⑤ More money needs to be spent protecting the coast.

34 What is the cartoonist's purpose in creating this cartoon?

① to convince people to move out of Louisiana
② to convince people to spend more on education
③ to discuss the issues they read about in the newspaper
④ to alert people of the need to address coastal erosion
⑤ to entertain his readers by presenting absurd ideas

Questions 35 and 36 refer to the following political cartoon.

35 What is the cartoonist trying to do in the above cartoon?

① contrast Brazil's escape from oil dictators to the dependence of the U.S. on the use of oil
② point out the risk of the U.S. protecting oil dictators from competition with Brazil
③ show that oil dictators have too much influence and power over the economy of the U.S.
④ highlight how Brazil's independence from the use of oil is fueling its economic growth and prosperity
⑤ alert the reader that the oil dictators of the Middle East are trying to control the world's economy

36 Which of the following is implied in the above cartoon?

① If the U.S. continues with its current policies, it will continue to flourish.
② For the stability of its economy, the U.S. needs to take control of oil producing areas.
③ The U.S. would benefit from following Brazil's lead in escaping from our dependence on oil.
④ The U.S. needs to consider Brazil a serious competitor in the world marketplace.
⑤ Oil dictators control the U.S. economy because we depend on foreign oil.

Questions 37 and 38 refer to the following photograph.

37 The above photograph is of a pioneer family in Nebraska in 1886. Given that information, what does the photograph tell us?

① The pioneers were able to easily travel in comfort.
② Pioneer men would send for their families after they were settled.
③ The pioneers did not want to be photographed.
④ The pioneers traveled with their families and all their belongings.
⑤ The pioneers traveled on horseback.

38 Which of the following is a fact?

① The bearded man appears to be a hard-working person.
② The family looks like they have had a difficult journey.
③ The clothing they are wearing was typical of the pioneers.
④ The family will probably settle at this location.
⑤ The family is well prepared for life on the prairie.

Questions 39 and 40 refer to the following photograph.

39 What value does the above photograph show?

① striving for material gain
② hard work
③ enjoying life
④ planning ahead
⑤ self-sacrifice

40 That photographer seems to be trying to persuade the viewer that

① it is important to always be planning for the future
② boys and girls shouldn't play together
③ children are wasting too much time playing
④ the children in the photograph are deprived
⑤ the simple joys of life are the most precious

Question 41 is based on the following poster.

Make
levees,
not
war

41 According to the above poster, what was one cause of the flooding in New Orleans?

① spending resources on war instead of needed repairs
② people fighting each other instead of working together
③ poor workmanship on the levees that should protect the city
④ a major hurricane more powerful than ever anticipated
⑤ necessary levees that were needed were never built

Questions 42 and 43 are based on the following bar graph.

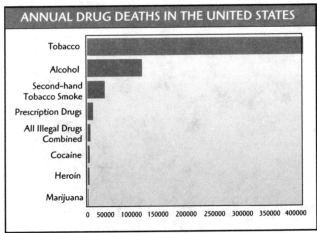

Source: National Institute on Drug Abuse

42 If our national priority were to save lives while preserving our freedom of choice, how would we apply the information given in this graph?

① outlaw tobacco and alcohol use and enforce the ban with long prison terms
② increase funding and personnel for the war on illegal drugs
③ legalize all illegal drugs and sell them over the counter
④ spend more on tobacco and alcohol use prevention programs
⑤ legalize all types of advertising for tobacco and alcohol products

43 According to the graph, the drug that is responsible for the most drug deaths in the United States is

① tobacco
② alcohol
③ cocaine
④ heroin
⑤ marijuana

Questions 44 and 45 are based on the following table.

CHILE IN THE INTERNATIONAL PACKAGED SOFTWARE MARKET (IN US $ MILLIONS)		
	1994	1998
Chilean Exports	38.8	170.7
World Sales	77,492.0	121,489.0
Chilean Share of World Sales	0.05%	0.14%
Total Latin-American Sales (exc. Chile)	1,764.9	3,051.0
Chilean Software Sales in Latin-America	23.7	102.0
Chilean Share of Sales in Latin-America	1.3%	3.3%

44 The data in the above table shows that

① Chile has more software sales than any other Latin American country
② by 2002, Chilean exports should exceed 300 million dollars
③ Brazil is the major competitor of Chile in software sales in Latin America
④ Chile's share of sales in Latin America peaked in 1998
⑤ there is a trend of growth for Chilean software sales in Latin America

45 There is enough information in this table to determine that

① the Chilean share of world sales is projected to exceed 1% by 2010
② the Chilean share of sales in Latin America rose about 2% from 1994 to 1998
③ by 1998, the Chilean economy had overheated and needed a correction
④ Chilean exports were the main source of software sales in Argentina
⑤ the Chilean software industry is the most productive and profitable in Latin America

Questions 46 and 47 are based on the following bar graph.

WHEAT EXPORTS 2003/2004		
Country	Amount	
United States	28,500 thousand metric tons	
Australia	15,000 thousand metric tons	
Canada	14,500 thousand metric tons	
Argentina	9,000 thousand metric tons	
Kazakhstan	6,500 thousand metric tons	
Russia	3,500 thousand metric tons	
India	2,000 thousand metric tons	
Turkey	800 thousand metric tons	
Ukraine	100 thousand metric tons	
Total:	8,877.8 thousand metric tons	

46 What is the best summary of the main idea of the above graph?

① Many nations export wheat to other nations around the world.
② The U.S., Australia, and Canada account for most wheat exports.
③ Most wheat is sold and used locally rather than exported to other nations.
④ The U.S. exported 28,500 thousand metric tons of wheat from 2003 to 2004.
⑤ India, which used to have to import food, is now a major wheat exporter.

47 This graph suggests that

① English-speaking nations do a better job of growing and exporting wheat
② there is enough food produced worldwide to alleviate world hunger
③ more countries should be involved in the wheat export market
④ if Russia adopted modern farming techniques, it could produce more wheat
⑤ subsidies (government payments) to U.S. farmers affect the price of wheat sold on the international market

Question 48 is based on the following table.

TOP 10 CITIES OF THE YEAR 1000	
Name	Population
1 Cordova, Spain	450,000
2 Kaifeng, China	400,000
3 Constantinople (Istanbul), Turkey	300,000
4 Angkor, Cambodia	200,000
5 Kyoto, Japan	175,000
6 Cairo, Egypt	135,000
7 Baghdad, Iraq	125,000
8 Nishapur (Neyshabur), Iran	125,000
9 Al-Hasa, Saudi Arabia	110,000
10 Patan (Anhilwara), India	100,000

48 Which of the following is an unstated assumption about information in the above table?

(1) The larger the city, the better place it is to live in.
(2) The population of all the world's cities in 1000 is known.
(3) Once a city becomes a top city, it tends to remain a top city.
(4) The top cities of the year 1000 were located in Europe.
(5) The top cities were all located in the most powerful states and empires.

Questions 49 and 50 are based on the following bar graph.

MURDERS WITH FIREARMS 1998–2000		
Country	Amount	
1 South Africa	31,918	
2 Colombia	21,898	
3 Thailand	20,032	
4 United States	8,259	
5 Mexico	3,589	
6 Zimbabwe	598	
7 Germany	384	
8 Belarus	331	
9 Czech Republic	213	
10 Ukraine	173	
11 Poland	166	
12 Canada	165	
13 Costa Rica	126	
14 Slovakia	117	
15 Spain	97	
16 Uraguay	84	
17 Portugal	84	
18 Lithuania	83	
19 Bulgaria	63	
20 United Kingdom	62	

49 The United States has by far the most murders with firearms of any developed, Western nation. The most probable cause of this is

(1) the lack of adequate law enforcement in the U.S.
(2) the great difference between rich and poor in the U.S.
(3) the American media's glamorization of violence
(4) the ease of buying and owning guns in the U.S.
(5) the lack of understanding the value of a human life in the U.S.

50 What is a value that might be measured by the information in this table?

① the respect for human life
② the importance of saving face
③ the concern for relationships
④ devotion to religious beliefs
⑤ right to privacy

Posttest Evaluation Chart

After you complete the GED Posttest, check your answers with the Answer Key on page 159. Then use this chart to figure out which skills you need to review. In column 1, circle the numbers of the questions you missed. The second, third, and fourth columns tell you the name and number of each skill and the pages to review. From the fifth column, use the pages from Contemporary's *GED Social Studies* for further practice, if necessary.

Question Number	Skill Name	Skill	Pages	GED Social Studies
5	Restating Information	1	20–21	33–38
1	Summarizing the Main Idea	2	22–23	27–32
7	Identifying Implications	3	24–25	39–42
2	Applying Given Ideas	4	26–29	43–52
3	Applying Remembered Ideas	5	30–31	53–58
13	Distinguishing Facts from Opinions and Hypotheses	6	32–33	59–64
10	Drawing Conclusions	7	34–35	65–70
18	Recognizing Persuasive Language	8	36–37	71–72
9	Recognizing Unstated Assumptions	9	38–39	73–78
14	Identifying Cause and Effect Relationships	10	40–41	79–83
15	Recognizing the Writer's Point of View	11	42–43	84–87
8	Recognizing the Historical Context of a Text	12	44–45	88–91
6	Identifying Comparisons and Contrasts	13	46–47	92–94
16	Judging Information	14	48–49	99–101
4	Recognizing Values	15	50–51	102–104
12	Judging the Adequacy of Facts	16	52–53	105–109
11	Comparing and Contrasting Different Viewpoints	17	54–55	110–112
17	Identifying Faulty Reasoning	18	56–57	113–118
23	Restating Map Information	19	58–59	119–122, 293
24	Identifying Implications	20	60–61	7, 138–139, 295–296
27	Applying Map Information	21	62–63	161–165, 334, 336–337
25	Identifying the Purpose and Use of a Map	22	64–65	290, 298
19	Identifying Comparisons and Contrasts	23	66–67	119, 293
20	Applying Given Ideas	24	68–69	314–315
22	Judging the Adequacy of Facts	25	70–71	160–161, 343

Question Number	Skill Name	Skill	Pages	GED Social Studies
21	Drawing Conclusions	26	72–73	16, 153, 177, 301, 334
26	Distinguishing Fact from Opinion	27	74–75	336–337
33	Summarizing the Main Idea	28	76–77	6, 281
36	Identifying Implications	29	78–79	20, 321
32	Applying Remembered Ideas	30	80–81	173, 346–347
37	Applying Given Ideas	31	82–83	345–347
38	Distinguishing Fact from Opinion	32	84–85	345
40	Recognizing Persuasive Information	33	86–87	302–303
34	Understanding the Photographer's or Cartoonist's Purpose	34	88–89	196–198, 351
30	Recognizing Unstated Assumptions	35	90–91	244
41	Identifying Cause and Effect Relationships	36	92–93	181
29	Recognizing the Cartoonist's or Photographer's Point of View	37	94–95	11
28	Recognizing Historical Context	38	96–97	175–176
35	Identifying Comparisons and Contrasts	39	98–99	151–152
31	Recognizing Values	40	100–101	312, 338
39	Determining the Implications and Effects of Values	41	102–103	11, 338, 349
44	Recognizing a Trend in Data	42	104–105	178, 223, 229–230, 277
46	Summarizing the Main Idea	43	106–107	187–188, 226, 340–341
47	Identifying Implications	44	108–109	131–132, 154, 249, 291–292
42	Applying Information Given	45	110–111	17, 128–129, 200–201, 227, 274–275, 316
48	Recognizing Unstated Assumptions	46	112–113	171, 214
45	Judging the Adequacy of Facts	47	114–115	18, 243, 352
49	Identifying Cause and Effect Relationships	48	116–117	128–130, 171
43	Identifying Comparisons and Contrasts	49	118–119	17, 251, 263, 348
50	Recognizing Values	50	120–121	274–275, 322

Answer Key

Pretest

1 ① The first sentence gives the main idea that the 1960s was the great era of African independence. The rest of the passage gives additional details to support this main idea.

2 ③ By calling the 1960s the great era of African independence, the author makes clear that he considers the gaining of independence by all of these African nations to be very important.

3 ③ Fewer horses were needed in the early twentieth century. Therefore, there was less of a need for those who took care of the needs of horses. Since fewer horseshoes were needed, there was less of a need for blacksmiths.

4 ② The change from the horse to machinery was driven by a desire to have more productivity and efficiency. People wanted to get more done with less effort.

5 ③ The dollar is circulated in 87 percent of countries, while the euro is circulated in 27 percent. The sum of these two percentages is greater than 100 percent. Therefore, there are some countries where both the dollar and euro are circulating.

6 ⑤ Currency is money. The euro is money, just like the dollar is.

7 ⑤ The writer opposes the Revolution. He is loyal to the British king. He wants the reader to share his views.

8 ④ A British sympathizer would express the British point of view. This passage appears to be written at the time of the American Revolution.

9 ② Union soldiers were fighting to preserve the Union, while Confederate soldiers were fighting for the right of their states to secede, or leave the United States.

10 ④ British and French soldiers were evenly matched. They were loyal to their countries, fought bravely, and suffered tremendously.

11 ① Since the atomic bomb has not been used in warfare for over 60 years, it is hard to claim that it changed warfare forever.

12 ④ The Japanese fought very bravely and well. They were overwhelmed by the huge numerical and material superiority of the Allies.

13 ⑤ Shingarev does not regret the Revolution, but he knows that people are suffering because of it.

14 ② By his statement, Lenin makes clear that he does not believe in democracy. He appears to assume that nationwide terror and destruction are the path to Soviet greatness.

15 ⑤ By saying, "Long live Yugoslavia! Long live peace and brotherhood," he appears to be supporting all the people, not just Serbs.

16 ③ When he argues that Serbia has a right to Kosovo, he ignores the fact that 90 percent of the people are Albanians, not Serbs.

17 ① Poland joining the European Union is an example of internationalism, or working cooperatively with other nations.

18 ② It is an opinion that nationalism should be opposed by reasonable people. It is possible to gather evidence to support all of the other statements.

19 ① While the U.S. had the largest number of Nobel prizes, this does not necessarily mean that it had the best science education system.

20 ① Almost all of the scientific Nobel Prizes were awarded to the United States or Europe. This indicates that those two regions were the world centers of innovation.

21 ④ The most important purpose of a ski map is to help skiers select a lift and trail appropriate to their ability. That is why every trail is labeled *easiest*, *intermediate*, or *expert*.

22 ⑤ An expert skier would want to spend most of the day using lifts 2 and 5, since they lead to the expert trails.

23 ⑤ The greatest contrast was in the exploration of Africa, where Portugal explored the entire coast while Spain did not explore at all.

24 ③ There is no information on the map that indicates the future success of the British.

25 ① The trend nationwide is clearly toward more prisons. If Nevada is rapidly growing, it will need more prisons soon.

26 ③ It is an opinion that the number of prisoners is a national disgrace. All the other statements can be proved with information from the maps.

27 ④ Given the unbroken hundred-year trend, it is likely that the number of prisons will continue to increase.

28 ④ The details of the calls being tracked make it clear that the NSA collection of phone records of ordinary Americans makes no sense.

29 ② The cartoon is commenting on the fact that the NSA had been collecting details of the phone records of ordinary Americans.

30 ④ The style of the cars and the clothes of the millionaires dates them in the 1930s.

31 ① The humor is having millionaires circling their limousines as if they were pioneers in a wagon train circling the wagons at night for protection.

32 ② The employer is hiring someone who looks like his double.

33 ③ The cartoonist does not believe that hiring someone exactly like yourself is such a good idea. By making the employer so delighted with his double, he makes it appear that all he wants is to keep the status quo.

34 ⑤ It was assumed that the color "flesh" was the color of an average Caucasian. This cartoon points out that human flesh comes in all sorts of colors.

35 ③ The cartoonist makes the diverse group look very innocent, patient, and nonthreatening. It is obvious that they all expect to be served. The cartoonist is trying to convince his reader that the old view of what "flesh colored" means is not acceptable.

36 ④ The employer is dressed in a pirate costume. The cartoonist expects the reader to know what a pirate looks like and what he does.

37 ① The boss is a pirate who is saying, "Welcome aboard." The new worker will probably be expected to become a pirate as well.

38 ③ The advertisement is trying to convince the reader to buy land or a home in Shorewood Park. It gives the price of land and the price of a bungalow while describing the advantages of the neighborhood.

39 ② Even though people were attracted to Shorewood, San Francisco was growing rapidly enough at the time that other neighborhoods were not badly hurt by Shorewood Park's growth.

40 ⑤ The photograph shows very clearly that separate but equal was anything but a reality.

41 ⑤ At the time, in the South, there was officially sanctioned separation of the races, or segregation. Many people at the time considered this a positive value, though today we consider it misguided or worse.

42 ① The line for overall drug use declines starting in 1978 and continuing until 1993.

43 ① The percentage of high school seniors who reported using marijuana is almost the same as the total amount of illegal drug users. If marijuana were legalized, those students who only used marijuana would no longer be counted as illegal drug users. As a result, the total percentage of illegal drug use would drop.

44 ⑤ The top four and eight out of the top ten slave-holding states were southern states. The other two were border states. Well over 90 percent of all slaves lived in the South.

45 ⑤ Of the five choices, Connecticut is the only one the chart says had no slavery. The chart does not list Texas or Florida.

46 ③ All of the non-white components of the state population are growing at a faster percentage rate than the white population. This will continue to make the state more diverse.

47 ① Per capita income data is not needed in order to make a prediction of which group will be larger in the state in the future.

48 ① The table makes no assumptions about the prosperity of any of these urban areas.

49 ④ This table compares populations, not importance, of these urban areas.

50 ① People most often move to a city in order to better themselves or their families. The growth of these urban areas reflects people's commitment to this value.

Skill 1

1 Since the opposite of an adversarial relationship is described later in the passage as a strengthened relationship, you can conclude that an adversarial relationship is an antagonistic or hostile relationship.

2 A country's domestic policies deal with what is going on inside the country.

GED Practice

1 ④ A stabilizing labor market is a steady one, with jobs and workers in balance.

2 ③ *Muted* means subdued. In other words, very little change is happening.

3 ② The examples show that a modern name for a muckraker would be an investigative reporter.

4 ⑤ The last paragraph states that new laws were passed as a result of the public's reaction to the muckrakers' work.

Skill 2

1 Your summary should be similar to "Though founded on a discovery of gold, Georgetown became the greatest silver producer in the world." This summary expresses the main idea of the passage.

GED Practice

1 ④ The passage gives examples of both rights and responsibilities.

2 ③ The passage lists the major contributions of the Sumerians to world civilization.

3 ⑤ The passage describes the separation of powers. The key thought is that this separation of powers exists to protect the freedom of Americans.

Skill 3

1 The writer mentions mutual accusations of hostility. The implication is that both sides were responsible for the Cold War.

2 When Winston Churchill used the image of an "iron curtain," he was implying that the countries of Eastern Europe were being imprisoned by the Soviet Union.

GED Practice

1 ⑤ The desire to have a better life was more important to an individual settler than any other idea. While spreading democracy might have been important to Americans as a whole, the settlers usually had more practical and personal reasons for going.

2 ② Today, calling Native Americans incapable of self-government would be considered racist and wrong.

③ **⑤** Carrie Fulton Phillips was willing to make her affair public. She was ready to harm Harding's chance of becoming president unless she was paid off.

④ **②** It is reasonable to conclude that there would have been a public uproar if the affair had become public. It is also reasonable to conclude that knowledge of the affair would have cost Harding votes. The Republican Party believed this and was willing to pay for Phillips's silence.

Skill 4

① The inheritance tax is the most progressive because it is only paid by the wealthy. Poor and middle-class people pay nothing at all.

② The graduated income tax is the next most progressive because wealthier people are taxed at a higher rate.

③ The property tax is the next most progressive because some people, such as the elderly, might own property, but not have the income to maintain it.

④ The lottery is the most regressive tax because mostly poor and lower-income people buy the lottery tickets in hope of winning a large amount of money.

Special GED Item Type

① Amendment 5 would apply. Simpson cannot be tried twice for the same crime.

② Amendment 6 would apply. The accused have not been informed of the charges against them and they are not getting a speedy trial.

③ Amendment 1 would apply. The Native Americans want to practice their religion.

GED Practice

① **⑤** The Ayatollah is a religious ruler who has the political power to rule.

② **②** Kim Jong Il rules his nation by the threat of force.

③ **④** South Africa is a representative democracy. It has free elections and more than one political party.

④ **③** The Turkish man is outside of his country. Due to his torture, he has reason to fear for his safety. He also has good reason not to trust the Turkish government. None of the other choices meet all three criteria.

⑤ **②** Cortez wanted the gold of the Aztecs.

⑥ **①** The Pilgrims were mostly motivated by the desire for religious freedom.

⑦ **⑤** The Franciscans were missionaries. They wanted to convert the Hopi to Christianity.

⑧ **①** Just like the descendents of William the Conqueror became British, the descendents of Genghis Khan became Chinese.

Skill 5

① In 2005, Hurricane Katrina was an environmental disaster that had an impact similar to the Dust Bowl.

② Both disasters resulted in thousands of people losing their homes and their livelihood. Both were major environmental disasters. Differences include the hurricane causing damage from flooding, while the Dust Bowl was caused by drought causing damage from dust. Also, in the 1930s, there was little help for the victims of the Dust Bowl. In 2005, after a terrible start, some help was given to many of the victims of the hurricane.

GED Practice

① **③** The United States Constitution is the basis for law in the United States. The Code of Hammurabi was the basis for law in ancient Babylonia.

② **①** Like the Asians and Africans trying to enter Europe, illegal immigrants from Mexico face danger trying to enter the United States. Once they succeed in entering, they also face problems working legally, getting medical care, and getting legal protection.

③ ③ Mecca is the destination for Muslim pilgrims just like Varanasi is the destination for Hindu pilgrims.

④ ④ Once they were driven out of Jerusalem, the Jewish people also had to face the challenge of keeping their religion alive while far away from their homeland.

Skill 6

① **F** By checking census data, you can confirm that California, Texas, New York, and Florida have the greatest number of immigrants.

② **O** It is an opinion, or statement of the writer's feelings, that the states were extremely fortunate.

③ **H** This hypothesis can be tested by looking at data of the number of immigrants of each state and the economic growth of each state.

④ **F** By checking tax records, this statement can be proved.

⑤ **F** By checking the background of workers in low-paying, undesirable jobs, this statement can be proved.

⑥ **H** This hypothesis can be tested by setting up controlled experiments.

⑦ **O** The writer is expressing personal feelings.

GED Practice

① ⑤ It is an opinion of the author that Europe became a better place to live because of the Renaissance. The works of Michelangelo, da Vinci, and Raphael are so accepted as great works of art that this can be considered a fact rather than an opinion.

② ① Only choice number one offers a reason that can be tested for what might have been a cause of the Renaissance.

③ ④ James Brady was shot in 1981. In 1993, 12 years later, the Brady Bill became law.

Skill 7

① A reasonable conclusion would be that Vietnam's policy to drive out the French was unsuccessful.

② Evidence in the passage includes the statement that Thailand was the only nation in Southeast Asia that was never a colony. Since Vietnam is in Southeast Asia, you can draw the conclusion that Vietnam became a colony of France. The passage also gives as reasons for Thailand's success its developing relationships with many Western nations. Vietnam only had a relationship with one, France. Also, while the King of Siam tried to modernize his country, Vietnam resisted Western influence.

GED Practice

① ④ The first tribal college was founded based on the belief that education would help members of the tribe. In less than 40 years, more than 30 more of these tribal colleges were founded. In addition, some of these institutions have grown into colleges and universities. They have also attracted important donors including the Bill and Melinda Gates Foundation and the American Indian College Fund. This is all evidence that the colleges are making a difference on their reservations.

② ② The single most important piece of evidence is that so many colleges have been founded in less than 40 years. This suggests that the success of the first tribal colleges encouraged other tribes to start their own.

③ ① The Marshall Plan was a great example of the success of helping nations help themselves.

Skill 8

① The phrases "right to a good death" and "basic human freedom" are meant to convince you that physician-assisted suicide is a good idea. Words and phrases like "unbearable pain," "suffer," and "treated cruelly" all create an image of a life of misery.

② The phrases "culture of life" and "value human life" are meant to persuade you that ending a life is wrong. Phrases like "culture of death" and "greedy relatives eager to get their wealth" make physician-assisted suicide seem like a bad idea.

GED Practice

❶ ① The writer is opposed to the European Union constitution in its current form.

❷ ④ Warm and cold water use less energy than hot water.

❸ ③ The writer makes it clear that he is a supporter of Robert Mugabe. He is trying to convince his reader that his view is accurate.

Skill 9

❶ There are a number of unstated assumptions made by President Bush. One is that attacking Iraq would distract terrorists from attacking the U.S. Another is that invading Iraq prevented another attack in the U.S. A third assumption is that terrorists were based in Iraq to begin with.

GED Practice

❶ ③ The usual assumption is that a much smaller army would be defeated.

❷ ② The policy of Neville Chamberlain was called appeasement. The idea was that giving in to an aggressive dictator would satisfy him, ending all conflict. The assumption turned out to be wrong.

❸ ⑤ The writer points out that politicians can find out who voted and who didn't. By saying that as a result, the nonvoter is a loser, the writer assumes that the politician will be more concerned with a person who votes. The reason for that is because that person will most likely vote in the next election.

④ ⑤ The one assumption that mutual assured destruction did not make is that a nuclear nation might collapse and lose control of its weapons. But that is what happened when the Soviet Union collapsed. We still do not know if all of the former Soviet weapons are accounted for.

Skill 10

❶ Causes of the American Revolution included actions by the British like the Navigation Acts, the Stamp Tax, the tax on tea, and the occupation of Boston. Causes also include actions by the colonists such as the speeches by James Otis against the Navigation Acts, the Boston Tea Party, and the creation of the Continental Congress.

❷ Some common themes include British attempts to raise money from the colonists by taxation and the colonists increasing resistance to those attempts.

GED Practice

❶ ③ High income and inheritance taxes might have improved the distribution of wealth. The unequal distribution of wealth was a major cause of the Great Depression.

❷ ② When there is too much supply of an item, its price goes down.

❸ ④ Rather than being grateful, the Taliban thought the United States was an enemy of Islam. It provided safe haven to Al-Qaeda, which carried out terrorist attacks against the United States.

Skill 11

1 The time period is the mid-nineteenth century around 1850. The clues are that the travelers are described as California adventurers and that California is described as the land of gold. The California Gold Rush began in 1849. Further evidence of the time period is that they had to take a ferry to get across the Hudson River. A railroad bridge had not yet been built across the river.

2 They were going to California. They were expecting to get rich by finding gold.

GED Practice

1 ① The writer states, "We are still trying to get ourselves called just 'pilots.'"

2 ④ By this time, planes were becoming more reliable and were capable of cross-country flights. But these flights were still new enough to be considered an event.

3 ⑤ The writer states that, "*The Post's* city editor woke me at home and asked me to come in to cover an unusual burglary."

4 ③ The descriptions of his actions indicate that the writer was just trying to pursue the story and get the truth.

Skill 12

1 Both passages describe Native Americans before the arrival of Europeans.

2 The first passage describes Native Americans as very primitive. It blames faults in their character for their conquest by Europeans. The second passage describes the advanced and diverse nature of Native Americans before the arrival of Europeans. It focuses on the agricultural innovations of the Native Americans.

3 The cultural sensitivity shown in the second passage is typical of the period since the 1950s. The passage was written after 1960.

GED Practice

1 ① References to temples in which sacrifices are offered and deities or gods chose women to serve them places this account in ancient times. Marduk was the leading god of Babylon. Darius and Xerxes were rulers of ancient Persia.

2 ② Herodotus, the writer of this account, relates as fact that the god himself chose a woman to stay at his temple. This would not be believed as true today.

3 ② The writer met Miss Adams in 1900.

4 ④ Brigham Young, the leader of the Mormons, led the effort to build the theater.

Skill 13

1 Every one of these racial and ethnic groups was either guilty or a victim of genocide.

2 These groups came from different races, religions, and parts of the earth.

GED Practice

1 ④ The Chinese do not have true choices in their elections.

2 ② Almost every red state remained red in the second presidential election, and almost every blue state remained blue.

Skill 14

1 One flaw in this argument is that the federal government represents all the people of the United States, not just the states. Another flaw is that a state does not have the right to discriminate against some of its citizens. Rather than oppressing a law-abiding state, what the federal government was doing was trying to prevent African Americans from being oppressed in southern states.

GED Practice

❶ ③ In this case, the Palestinian vote appears to contradict the claim that people will elect governments that want to get along with their neighbors.

❷ ② In this case, the customer is not paying the best price. These customers appear to be more influenced by the desire to purchase from a prestigious store than by the law of supply and demand.

❸ ① The Aswan High Dam is a huge public works project that is an enormous benefit to its country. There are negative side effects of the dam, but today it is the major source of electricity for Egypt.

Skill 15

❶ The values that motivated the first Crusaders included the desire to defend Christian society and pilgrimages to Jerusalem.

GED Practice

❶ ③ Life, liberty, and the pursuit of happiness can all be considered human rights.

❷ ① Since the museum respects all native cultures, its main value is multiculturalism.

❸ ④ Even though he was a leader of the American Revolution, John Adams defended the British soldiers. The main value he was following was justice, or making sure that everyone was treated fairly and equitably.

Skill 16

❶ We must determine whether the new peanut butter and jelly sandwich is a completely new product or an important improvement of another product. Most importantly, we need to determine whether or not it is just an obvious change from the traditional peanut butter and jelly sandwich.

❷ The argument for granting the patent is that no one ever thought of patenting this before and that it is a significant improvement because it would be less messy than the traditional sandwich. The argument against granting the patent is that with the enormous popularity of pita pockets, this innovation is just an obvious change.

GED Practice

❶ ② The passage gives no evidence to support the claim that Rockefeller used dishonest and unfair methods.

❷ ② This is a broad claim that cannot be fully supported by the passage.

Skill 17

❶ They might have focused more on the faults of the people they conquered. They might have written about being discriminated against. They might have considered the well-off towns greedy and selfish. They also might have considered them cowardly and weak. They would differ from the accounts we have today because they would have been written from a totally different point of view.

❶ ② The National Party was dominated by the Afrikaners, the descendants of the Dutch settlers. Evidence in the passage includes the references to self-determination. The creation of the black mini-states is described in the context of allowing self-determination of the separate groups in South Africa.

❷ ④ The African National Congress was dominated by black militants who wanted to end the oppression of their people by the white minority. They understood apartheid to be a form of racism that attempted to dehumanize the black majority and marginalize the other non-white people.

Skill 18

❶ His error in logic is assuming that because the Japanese nation is an enemy of the United States, everyone whose ancestors are from there are also enemies. The crudest expression of his prejudice is his claim that "A Jap's a Jap."

❷ In studying racism in the United States, an important question would be how German Americans and Italian Americans were treated. Even though we were at war with Germany and Italy as well as with Japan, no attempt was made to move either German Americans or Italian Americans to internment camps.

GED Practice

❶ ④ Unfortunately, the record does show that President Bush has distorted the truth, though there is some dispute as to whether that has happened intentionally.

❷ ④ Ridge did not represent the vast majority of Cherokee. Only a small minority supported him.

Skill 19

❶ The series of maps shows the rapid urbanization and sprawl of the Las Vegas area.

GED Practice

❶ ② According to the map, Coronado was the only explorer that covered the West. The other explorers covered east and central North America.

❷ ③ The line on the map representing the Silk Road links Xian, a city in China, to Antioch, a city in the Middle East.

❸ ① There is no evidence on this map that the Arab Muslim Empire was the most powerful in the world in 750. Much of the world is not shown on this map.

Skill 20

❶ An implication of this map is that it is getting warmer in the Arctic.

GED Practice

❶ ② These nations all have the longest life expectancy. A reasonable implication is that they have the best health care, since people live longer.

❷ ③ The map shows that the North had far more rail lines and that the system was more complete. This gave the North a huge advantage in transportation.

Skill 21

❶ The fastest route would be to take Route 25 North to Route 70 West. Another alternative would be to take Route 24 West to Route 70 West, but this would probably not be as fast as taking interstate highways for the entire trip.

GED Practice

❶ ③ According to the weather map, you can expect rain in Southern California.

❷ ① Zone A has the lowest annual heating costs in every fuel category.

❸ ① According to the map, upper New York State is in Zone D. The average annual heating cost for gas in that zone is $754.

Skill 22

1 ① The map could be used to identify the extent of Greek colonization from 750 to 500 B.C. It also identifies the different cities, tribes, and ethnic groups in and around the Greek colonies.

GED Practice

1 ① The map could be used to plan water usage, because it can provide an early warning of a drought or a water shortage.

2 ⑤ This map could be used to identify the first civilizations to develop. These civilizations would likely be the first to produce food.

Skill 23

1–**4** Answers will vary. For example, California, Illinois, and New York have a similar per capita income. Massachusetts and New Jersey would be states with a higher per capita income. Louisiana and Mississippi would have a lower per capita income.

GED Practice

1 ① Belmopan has an elevation between 0 and 1,000 feet. Washington, D.C., is the only choice in that range.

2 ③ The map shows that Canada still has most of its ancient forest. It also shows that most forest in the United States is not ancient forest.

Skill 24

1 Because of the high amount of water use, the farmer in Texas can assume that his or her area suffers from exceptional drought. The farmer should be concerned about his or her growing season.

2 The tree farm owner is being told that conditions are normal in his or her area.

GED Practice

1 ③ With all of the faults in the area, an earthquake is likely sometime in the future. The public safety departments would be wise to plan for one.

2 ② Restoring the prairie throughout this area is not a practical goal. The area is one of the main food-producing regions of the United States, and needs to continue to fill that role.

Skill 25

1 Based on the map you can state that New York, Illinois, Texas, Florida, and California have the most fines owed to attorneys. You can also point to states like Montana, North and South Dakota, Iowa, and Nebraska as having the lowest fines owed to attorneys.

2 Additional information that might explain these results includes populations of the states and the number of attorneys based in each state. The level of compliance of attorneys' clients in each state would be another clue to the reasons some states have more fines owed to attorneys than others.

GED Practice

1 ④ The Eastern Forest Indians were by far the largest group in North America.

2 ④ The map is a road map and only has adequate information to show how best to travel between the cities on the map. The map cannot answer any of the other choices.

Skill 26

1 Based on the large glaciers, you can conclude that the climate is very cold. The Arctic Circle on the map is another clue that the climate is cold.

2 You can conclude that the Inuit are a people whose lifestyle has been adapted to the cold.

GED Practice

❶ ⑤ The map shows far more people killed in Russia than anywhere else in Europe.

❷ ② The area of highest population density on the population map closely correlates with the area of highest light pollution on the light pollution map.

Skill 27

❶ fact

❷ opinion

❸ fact

❹ opinion

❺ fact

GED Practice

❶ ① It is an opinion that military sonar should be severely restricted.

❷ ③ Which alliance was stronger is a matter of opinion that is not decided by the information in the map.

Skill 28

❶ The main idea of the photograph is that these young boys worked under terrible conditions at the coal mine.

GED Practice

❶ ④ The man who has "California" written on his hat is attacking the Chinese man by pulling his hair and whipping him.

❷ ② Though all of the other choices are conclusions that can be drawn from this photograph, stating that the survivors had been starved and mistreated is the best fit for the main idea.

Skill 29

❶ The cartoon implies that the Fox River is dirty or polluted.

❷ The cartoon implies that the plan to clean up the river is not going to work. The phrase "taken to the cleaners" means being fooled or taken advantage of.

GED Practice

❶ ② Uncle Sam is a common symbol for the United States. The gas hose is wrapped around his neck. It appears that he might get strangled by the hose.

❷ ① Many men have climbed on each of the locomotives. The pair in the center are shaking hands. What looks like a bottle of champagne is being passed from one locomotive to the other. All of this indicates that the men in the picture were well aware that they were at an important historic event.

Skill 30

❶ The cartoon is referring to the story of Pinocchio. When Pinocchio lies, his nose grows longer and longer.

❷ The cartoonist wants you to believe that the cigarette company executives are lying.

GED Practice

❶ ② If the men were supporters of the new president, they would be celebrating. Instead they are "eating crow."

❷ ③ In the Bible, the four horsemen of the Apocalypse are supposed to bring about the end of the world. In the cartoon, spam, porn, viruses, and scams are bringing about the end of e-mail.

Skill 31

❶ Uncle Sam approves of Teddy Roosevelt.

❷ You would vote for Teddy Roosevelt for president.

GED Practice

❶ ② The cartoon shows a soldier on the left, and a "baby," or someone who has not enlisted in the war, on the right. The cartoon is meant to motivate the reader to be brave and join the army.

❷ ⑤ The man in the coffin looks natural because he is holding a remote and has a bag of chips. The message of the cartoon is to eat healthier and exercise more if you want to live.

Skill 32

❶ The cartoonist draws the inside of a prison cell. The caption for the prison cell is "Enron's New Executive Suite."

❷ The cartoonist's opinion is that the Enron executives are guilty and will end up in prison.

GED Practice

❶ ③ This fact is said by the man in the suit. All the other choices are opinions.

❷ ② The opinion that the cartoon is trying to promote is that giving women the vote will result in them neglecting their home and families. They would just want to be involved in politics.

Skill 33

❶ The photograph was able to persuade people around the world that the airplane had actually flown. Without a photograph, the Wright brothers might not have been believed.

GED Practice

❶ ① The images of men standing on the moon convinced people to support the space program.

❷ ④ When Americans saw this image and others from Pearl Harbor, it strengthened their resolve to go to war.

Skill 34

❶ When Samson's hair was cut, he lost his strength.

❷ The Modern Samson is all African Americans.

❸ His purpose was to say that by losing the right to vote, African Americans would lose all of their power.

GED Practice

❶ ③ The image shows the men to be heroic, patriotic, and triumphant.

❷ ① The cartoon shows the power of the Populist Party over the Democratic Party. The Populist snake with the head of William Jennings Bryan is swallowing the Democratic donkey.

Skill 35

❶ Herbert Block thought that Nixon was a sleazy character.

❷ He draws Nixon with stubble on his face. The assumption is that an unshaven man is not to be trusted. He also uses the image of Nixon climbing out of the sewer. Again, the assumption is that a sewer is dirty, and someone who comes out of a sewer is like a rat.

GED Practice

❶ ③ The 12-step program is the well-known method used by Alcoholics Anonymous to help people overcome alcohol addiction. Applying it to spending too much time on e-mail is funny because reading e-mail is not seen as being as threatening as alcoholism, yet many people are wasting too much time with e-mail.

❷ ① The unstated assumption of the cartoonist is that we do not have enough money to purchase good equipment for our troops. The impression is that it is the tax cut that is cutting into military spending. The cartoonist doesn't consider the possibility that we have plenty of money for the military, but might have misplaced priorities.

Skill 36

1 The high cost of a college education has to be paid for by parents. The exaggeration is that in order to pay for their child's education, these parents have given up everything, even their clothes.

GED Practice

1 ② What is being commented on is the use of performance-enhancing drugs by athletes.

2 ① The grenade can be expected to explode. When that happens, the economy, which is depicted as fragile eggs, will be wrecked.

Skill 37

1 The men in the boat are fearful of the income tax.

2 The cartoonist supports the income tax.

3 Drawing the income tax as a huge sea monster is evidence that the men in the boat should be afraid of it. Evidence of the cartoonist's point of view is the boat being labeled "Predatory Wealth," one of the men having dollar signs on his vest and a dollar sign in his hair, and two men clutching bags of money.

GED Practice

1 ④ The photographer appears to understand the importance of showing ordinary Russians leaning against the fallen statue of Dzerzhinsky. The image symbolizes the fall of communism in the Soviet Union.

2 ③ The many illegal immigrants seem to be having no difficulty climbing through holes in the border fence.

Skill 38

1 The woman is first putting on makeup and then welding.

2 These actions are taking place during World War II, when women, for the first time in large numbers, entered manufacturing jobs previously held only by men.

3 The evidence includes the subject matter of the cartoon, which shows that a woman using a welding machine is still considered new and unusual. The woman's clothing and makeup are also typical of the 1940s.

GED Practice

1 ④ Abraham Lincoln, who is holding the ax, was president during the Civil War. Also, slavery was a major issue of the Civil War.

2 ① The Taliban were extreme Islamic fundamentalists who ruled Afghanistan in 2001. They were particularly harsh in their treatment of women.

Skill 39

1 President Bush is being compared to Santa Claus.

2 The contrast is between the image of a kindly Santa Claus who just knows who is "naughty and nice" and President Bush in a Santa suit putting microphones down chimneys.

3 The cartoonist wants you to think that the NSA wiretap program authorized by President Bush is wrong. The cartoon is trying to convince you that the wiretaps are an invasion of privacy.

GED Practice

1 ⑤ "The war" has expensive clothes and appears very healthy and well-fed, while "U.S. urban needs" looks underfed and poorly dressed. "The war" is depicted as a glamorous kept woman who clearly has a lavish lifestyle. "U.S. urban needs" is depicted as an impoverished, neglected wife.

2 ② All of the other choices are illustrated in the contrast between the small older stone building in the foreground and the large modern towers in the background. Whether any of the buildings are dull or exciting is a matter of opinion.

Skill 40

① The generals appear to value power and authority.

② The cartoonist appears to believe in Christian values, especially in respecting the weak and the poor.

③ The generals are obviously not meek. When one of the generals describes his nightmare, he makes it clear that he does not want to give up his power and privilege. The cartoonist, by depicting the generals as so arrogant, and by having them contradict a basic well-known Christian belief, shows that his sympathy is with Christian values, not with the generals.

GED Practice

① ⑤ The agent assumes that the couple will value luxury over everything else.

② ① The family of the soldier expresses total love and joy.

Skill 41

① Limiting freedom could lead to the arbitrary imprisonments of a police state.

② The cartoonist does not appear to believe that this is a reasonable trade-off.

③ The contrast between the reasonable discussion of the caption and the very unreasonable image of the prisoners shackled to the wall shows that the cartoonist is trying to convey that what sounds reasonable could result in something very unreasonable.

GED Practice

① ④ The driver of the SUV is totally unwilling to change his lifestyle in any way. So the only way he can think of to control oil prices is to get more oil in any way possible.

② ① The driver of the alternative-energy vehicle appears ready to support any conservation measure.

③ ⑤ Because of militarism, or the desire to solve problems through military action, there was no one to help the people of Louisiana and Mississippi after Hurricane Katrina. The Louisiana and Mississippi national guardsmen were in Iraq instead.

Skill 42

① It is easier to figure out exact rates from a table.

② It is easier to see a trend with a graph.

③ After increasing from 1950 to 1965, the fertility rate has been declining ever since 1965.

GED Practice

① ① The time period of 1990 to 2000 is not the entire graph. During this ten-year period, the increase in per capita GNP was generally a steady increase. With only one year that showed a slight decrease out of ten years, the trend is still a steady increase.

② ③ The worldwide trend was to lose forest cover. Europe was the only region to gain forest cover. Although Africa was losing forest cover more rapidly than other regions, it was still following the general trend of losing forest cover.

③ ③ All countries except Europe show a decrease in forest cover.

Skill 43

① A full-time job for one wage earner at the minimum wage has never been enough money to get a family out of poverty.

② The bars never touch the poverty line. They are always below the poverty line.

GED Practice

① ⑤ The main idea is the comparison of the two countries.

② ④ The main story of this pie chart is that the Soviet Union's piece of the pie is larger than everyone else's put together. In other words, they lost more military than the rest of the Allies put together.

Skill 44

❶ An implication of the table is that by 2040 Hispanics will have become the major ethnic group in Texas.

GED Practice

❶ ② According to the carbon dioxide graph, the concentration of carbon dioxide is rapidly going up. The passage says most scientists believe this increase in concentration is causing global warming.

❷ ③ All of the ten fastest-growing metropolitan areas are in the South and West. Therefore, it seems likely that the South and West will continue to be the fastest-growing areas of the U.S.

Skill 45

❶ Because five of the top six oil producers are in the Middle East, the region is a very high priority for the U.S. A main reason the U.S. government is deeply involved in the Middle East is because it contains most of the world's oil reserves.

GED Practice

❶ ④ Only 3 percent of the new job growth was in transportation and storage, less than the other four choices.

❷ ② By far, motor vehicle accidents are the leading cause of death for young people. Spending less time in a car and driving defensively can reduce the risk. All the other choices reduce the risk of dying, but none have the impact of driving safely and less often.

Skill 46

❶ An unstated assumption of this graph is that teenagers will report honestly about their sexual activity.

GED Practice

❶ ③ The graph assumes that it is possible to figure out the amount of illegal drug purchases even though they are never reported. Suppliers and purchasers go to great lengths to hide this information from government officials.

❷ ⑤ The graph assumes that it is possible to predict future threats. Because these predictions are based on past experience, they are probably the best that can be projected. But these projections are not as reliable as measurements of the present or past.

Skill 47

❶ **N** Need to know the result of the 2008 Republican Convention.

❷ **A** Hillary Clinton was the leading candidate in March 2006.

GED Practice

❶ ⑤ The graph gives percent of change of energy consumption. It does not give actual amounts of consumption.

❷ ① The only question that the chart can answer of the five listed is how many personal computers per 1,000 people there were in Sweden in 2002. There were 622.5 computers per 1,000 people in Sweden in 2002.

Skill 48

❶ The cause and effect relationship is the prevalence of HIV/AIDS in the population and the number of orphans.

GED Practice

1 ④ Since China's trade is increasing so rapidly, it would have to have a greater impact on the economies of other countries.

2 ② The large increase in TV revenue would help pay for the even larger increase in player salaries.

Skill 49

1 From 1965 to 2001, the GNP per person in China was far lower than in the United States. The United States GNP per person was generally between 30 and 40 times larger than the GNP in China.

GED Practice

1 ② The Civil War had the highest percentage of Americans killed in action, 4.8 percent (Union and Confederate combined).

2 ④ World War II had more than 16 million Americans in the military, far more than any other conflict in American history.

3 ⑤ Prescription drugs make up 43 percent of out-of-pocket expenses, far more than any other cost.

Skill 50

1 The United States appears to value helping the rich at the expense of the poor.

GED Practice

1 ① Not a single nation reached the level of their pledge of 0.7 percent of GDP. Sweden came closest with 0.5 percent.

2 ① With a foreign aid rate of 0.5 percent of GDP, Sweden showed that it valued helping poor countries more than the other countries on the graph.

3 ③ India plants far more forests than it cuts down.

4 ④ Indonesia cuts 1,212 Ha of forest every year while replanting 0.1 Ha. That is the worst record of deforestation in Asia. By its actions, Indonesia appears to value maximizing forest exploitation.

GED Posttest

1 ⑤ The passage describes both the rise and fall of the dot-coms.

2 ② Tulip mania in Holland was most similar to the dot-coms. Fortunes were made overnight trading tulips just as people made fortunes investing in dot-coms. Fortunes were suddenly lost after the tulip crash, just as people were wiped out by the dot-com crash.

3 ③ A theocracy is rule by religious leaders. The Taliban were Islamic fundamentalists who governed according to an extreme version of Islam.

4 ④ The Taliban believed in an extreme application of Shari'ah, or Islamic law.

5 ② Chief Seattle is trying to explain that even if his people leave this land and die out, they will still be linked to the land. Their love of the land has made it sacred.

6 ① The American government believes that land can be bought and sold. Chief Seattle believes that land that has been lived upon is sacred and cannot be owned.

7 ③ Every generation will have differing needs and priorities. Therefore, there will always be a need for the political process and social movements.

8 ④ Young adults often have a greater tendency to be idealists and to be discontented with aspects of the world around them. They would be more likely to join social movements.

9 ① The tone of the entire passage indicates that the Industrial Revolution was a positive event, even though it is never directly stated.

10 ② The passage makes clear that it was the approach of innovation and invention, rather than a particular industry or invention like textiles and steam engines, that was the key to the Industrial Revolution.

11 ④ The passage makes clear that both sides see themselves as the injured party deprived of their rightful homeland.

12 ④ Given the depth of this conflict, leaders on both sides will have to show great courage to reach a solution.

13 ③ It is an opinion that guilds could have adjusted if they realized they had to. There is no way to test that opinion.

14 ⑤ New techniques and technology were the downfall of the guild system at the end of the medieval period.

15 ① She appears to be totally unaffected by the murder. She seems to see it as just one more interesting thing to write about.

16 ⑤ Louise Clappe makes it very clear that she knows that the arrested man was innocent.

17 ⑤ It is sound reasoning that the actions of the Janjaweed militia are a crime against humanity. Systematic rape, murder, and ethnic cleansing are valid criteria for determining crimes against humanity.

18 ④ The fact that the perpetrators of the violence are Arab and the victims are not is not in itself a reason to oppose the actions of the Sudanese government.

19 ② Of all the choices, Northern and Central Africa had the most nations under military rule for 24 or more years.

20 ② Industrialized nations did not have military governments. Most of Central Africa, where the Republic of the Congo was located, had military governments. Therefore, the Republic of the Congo was not an industrialized nation.

21 ① The map shows extensive areas of the earth with low population density. It is reasonable to conclude that more people could live in some of these areas.

22 ② You can use the map and the key to determine the population density of India. The other statements cannot be proved with this map.

23 ③ The map is titled, "Gadsden Purchase and Proposed Rail Routes: 1853." It clearly shows the route of the southern transcontinental railroad going through the Gadsden Purchase.

24 ① The map strongly implies that it was for economic reasons that the United States made the Gadsden Purchase.

25 ① The map clearly shows that large areas of the South were dependent on slaves for their agricultural production.

26 ② According to the map, cotton was planted over a far larger area than any of the other crops.

27 ⑤ The northern end of the trail is in Baxter State Park.

28 ⑤ Although the idea of an all-inclusive media center was considered a humorous extravagance in 1950, it is quite common today.

29 ② The cabinet for more home entertainment equipment is meant to be a joke. The cartoonist most likely believes that what is being sold is already wildly extravagant. One clue is that in 1950, color television was not being broadcast.

30 ② The humor is based on adding a date of founding to an elevation and a population, even though there is no reason to add these figures.

31 ③ By showing the board members in hot water in hell, the cartoonist is saying that they are paying for their dishonesty.

32 (5) The cartoonist expects the reader to recognize hell and know why people are supposed to be there.

33 (5) The newspaper headline is "Coastal Erosion." The man reading the newspaper is saying that eventually, Louisiana will erode away. This exaggeration is meant to point out the need to spend more to protect the coast.

34 (4) The cartoonist's purpose is to highlight the issue of coastal erosion threatening Louisiana.

35 (1) Brazil has made a major commitment to renewable fuels. The cartoonist shows Brazil escaping from the mouth of oil dictators in contrast to the U.S. continuing to depend on Middle Eastern oil.

36 (3) The cartoonist is depicting Brazil's energy independence as an example that the U.S. should follow.

37 (4) The photograph shows a pioneer family standing in front of their wagon, which contains all of their belongings.

38 (3) Whether their clothing was typical of the period is a fact that can be checked. All of the other statements are opinions.

39 (3) The children in the photograph appear to value enjoying life.

40 (5) The photographer captures wonderful expressions of joy on the faces of the children.

41 (1) The image of flooded New Orleans and the caption "Make levees, not war" shows the effect of devoting our national resources to war instead of to needed repairs to our cities, like levees.

42 (4) By far, the most deaths are from tobacco and alcohol use. Therefore, increasing funding for prevention programs would save lives. Outlawing the products and having long prison terms would be too extreme. Alcohol prohibition was tried before and it failed.

43 (1) According to the graph, deaths from tobacco and second-hand smoke are far greater than all other deaths from drugs combined.

44 (5) The data in the table shows a trend in the growth in Chilean software sales in Latin America. It grew from $23.7 million in 1994 to $102 million in 1998.

45 (2) According to the data in the table, the Chilean share of Latin American software sales grew from 1.3 percent in 1994 to 3.3 percent in 1998. That is a growth of 2 percent.

46 (2) The most important information on the graph is that the three nations at the top of the graph account for the majority of world wheat exports.

47 (5) Subsidies allow American farmers to sell their products at lower prices. Because the U.S. is the world's largest exporter, subsidies could have a great impact on world prices for wheat.

48 (2) The table assumes that the population figures from 1000 are known and reasonably accurate.

49 (4) Of all the causes given, the ease of getting a gun is probably the single most important cause for the large number of murders by firearms in the U.S.

50 (1) The respect for human life is the value that would appear to be measured by this table.

Glossary

apply ideas/information take information from a passage or graphic and use it in another situation

cause and effect relationship organization in a sentence or passage that gives the reason for an action or event and the result of that action or event. In a cartoon, the cause and effect are often exaggerated and must be inferred.

compare and contrast organization used by a writer or cartoonist to show how two or more things are alike or different

contour map a map that shows levels of elevation of the land

draw conclusions combine what you know with what you have read to figure out what the text means

fact a statement that can be proved. For example, *Austin is the capital of Texas* is a fact that can be proved.

faulty reasoning ways of thinking or believing that tend to lump ideas or people together and come up with inaccurate or prejudicial beliefs

hypothesis a possible explanation for an event or idea that can be tested to prove or disprove it

implication ideas that are suggested or implied in a passage, cartoon, or map but not stated directly

judge information read or listen to all of the information presented and decide which version of events is closer to the truth

main idea what the paragraph, passage, or graphic is trying to say about the topic. The main idea may be stated or it may be understood but unstated.

opinion a statement that expresses feelings, beliefs, or personal judgments. An opinion cannot be proved, but it can be supported with facts or statistics. For example, *Spring is the most beautiful season* is an opinion.

persuasive information/language writing, cartoons, or photos that attempt to influence your thinking and beliefs

point of view the perspective that a writer or cartoonist uses. The writer or cartoonist may use his or her particular bias about an event or idea.

prior knowledge knowledge of events, people, and ideas that you have learned from other readings or other situations

purpose the reason or intent that an author has when he or she creates a piece of writing, a cartoon, or a photograph

remembered ideas past events, stories, or people who are referred to in cartoons. In order to understand the cartoon, the reader must remember and understand the cultural references in the cartoon.

restate information use your own words to express an idea or describe something from a passage you have read or a map or cartoon you have seen

summarize restate a passage or the idea of a graphic, telling only the main idea. When you summarize, the summary is much shorter than the original passage.

topic what a paragraph or passage is about

trend a development or change shown by a graph or other data. A trend may show growth or decrease, improvement or deterioration.

unstated assumption a fact or statement that is taken for granted—that everyone should know or understand—but is not stated or given in the writing or cartoon. An unstated assumption may be well-founded or completely inaccurate.

values deeply held beliefs felt by a person or a culture

Index